Romeo and Juliet

ENJOY SHAKESPEARE

King Lear
Romeo and Juliet
Twelfth Night

Available Soon

Much Ado About Nothing

Check for new titles at www.FullMeasurePress.com

ENJOY SHAKESPEARE

Romeo and Juliet

By

William Shakespeare

A Verse Translation in English

By

Kent Richmond

Full Measure Press • Lakewood, California

Published by:
Full Measure Press
P.O. Box 6294
Lakewood, CA 90714-6294 USA

Online Orders: www.FullMeasurePress.com

© Copyright 2004 by Kent Richmond

All rights reserved. No part of this publication may be performed, reproduced, stored in a retrieval system, or transmitted in any form or by any means electronic, mechanical, photocopying, recording or otherwise, without the prior written permission of the author.

Library of Congress Control Number: 2004109446

ISBN, print ed.   0-9752743-1-7

First Printing

Printed in the United States of America

Contents

Illustrations

Front matter and page 145 illustrations from *Galerie des Personage de Shakspeare* (1844), compiled by Amédée Pichot (1795-1877). Paris: Baudry, Librairie Européenne. Front matter engraved by Audibran (b. 1810); page 144 engraved by Ch. Geoffroy.

Illustration on page 123 reprinted with permission of *Clipart.com* (© 2003 *www.clipart.com*).

Other illustrations from *Shakespeare in Pictorial Art* (1916) by Malcolm C. Salaman (text) and Charles Holme (ed.). London: "The Studio" Ltd. Page 14 from the drawing "O, Romeo, Romeo, Wherefore Art Thou Romeo?" by William Hatherell R.I. (1855-1920); page 19, detail from "Romeo and Juliet" by William Miller (1796-1882)/engraved by George Sigmund and John Gottlieb Facius; page 55, "Spranger Barry and Miss Nossiter as Romeo and Juliet (1759)" by R.Pyle/engraved by W. Elliott; page 87, detail from "In Friar Larwrence's Cell" by Henry Bunbury (1756-1811)/Engraved by J.J. Vandenbergh; page 166, by Rev. Matthew William Peters (1741/2-1814)/engraved by R.Rhodes.

Front cover photograph by Luke Richmond.

About this Translation

This translation makes the language of William Shakespeare's drama more contemporary without modernizing the play in any other way. No lines are omitted or simplified, and no characters or scenes are deleted.

My aim is for readers to experience Shakespeare's original with the level of challenge and comprehension offered to audiences 400 years ago. Despite the richness of the plays, theatergoers in that era did not need scene summaries to follow the plot, footnotes to interpret vocabulary, or elaborate gestures to help them recognize a joke or guess at the character's intentions or emotional state. After all, Shakespeare's characters tell us what they are thinking. The plays lasted a couple of hours, which means the actors spoke at a fairly rapid, though comfortable, pace.

To qualify this translation as authentic Shakespeare, I preserve the metrical rhythm of the original as much as possible. When the original employs iambic pentameter, this translation does too. When characters speak in prose, the translation shifts to prose. Rhymes, the occasional alliteration, and metrical irregularities are preserved. Jokes, inspired or lame, and poetic devices get equivalents in the modern language. Sentence length and syntactic complexity are the same.

No doubt this translation has changes that may disturb purists. For example, I abandon the distinction between *you* (formal/distant/deferential) and *thou* (familiar/condescending/insulting). For Elizabethan audiences, this distinction, although losing force in everyday speech, still revealed information about class level and speaker attitude. Today the distinction is obscure, and the use of *thou* achieves the opposite of Shakespeare's intention. For at least three hundred years the *Thou/thee/thy/thine* paradigm has been confined to

7

poetry, religious expression, and solemn, formal oratory. No matter how many reminders are offered, few modern readers will feel tension when a commoner addresses a noble as "thou" and may even misinterpret it as formal, elevated address. I have to signal disrespect in some other way. Remember that this translation wants the drama to come to life for modern audiences, not serve as a primer in the English of Queen Elizabeth I.

To help comprehension, I occasionally add brief pieces of exposition, careful to operate within the metrical constraints imposed by the original. Shakespeare sometimes makes references to Greek mythology and folk legends, many of which are obscure today. So "Toward Phoebus' lodging. Such a waggoner/As Phaeton...." becomes "to where the Sun God sleeps. Such a charioteer/His son...." This practice eliminates the need for footnotes, which are unavailable to the theater audience and a distraction to readers. The occasional endnote offers an alternate translation of a disputed passage or explains a decision to deviate from the original. Endnotes can be ignored without loss of comprehension.

I suggest reading the translation without referring to the original so that you can imagine the play as theater in real time with the rhythm and pacing undisturbed. Don't be surprised if the "colors" seem a bit brighter than you remember them. After four centuries, more than a little "linguistic grime" builds up as our language changes. Keep in mind how surprised we are when Renaissance paintings are restored to their original state and those muted, sepia hues turn into celebrations of color. My translation wants you to see the same colors that the groundlings and the royalty saw when they crowded into theaters 400 years ago.

I would like to thank my friends, colleagues, and family members for their support in this endeavor. At California State University, Long Beach, I received helpful comments and encouragement from Boak Ferris, Cheryl Chapman, Graham Thomas, Sue Cowan, Robert Berdan, and Richard

Spiese, along with University President Robert Maxson, Richard Manly, and the staff at the *Beachview* television show. Actor/director Daniel Cartmell and Professor Constance Orliski get credit for inviting me to many nights of live Shakespeare.

A special thanks goes to John McWhorter of the Manhattan Institute and the Linguistics Department at the University of California at Berkeley. His article "The Shakespearean Tragedy" in his book *The Word on the Street: Fact and Fiction about American English* put me onto the idea of doing complete and faithful verse translations of Shakespeare's plays.

Finally, I have received nothing but encouragement from my wife Lynne, my proofreader and first fan, and my sons Nate, Jeremy, and Luke.

Kent Richmond

Notes on the Meter

Shakespeare's plays mix blank verse (unrhymed iambic pentameter), prose, and songs. They also include couplets or other rhyme schemes to close scenes and heighten dramatic exchanges. This translation preserves these forms, assuming Shakespeare had a dramatic justification for these swings between blank verse, prose, and rhyme.

In translating songs, I mimic the rhythm and find suitable rhymes, but Shakespeare's iambic pentameter is more problematic and requires decisions as to what constitutes a metrical line. His plays, especially the later ones, are full of short lines, long lines, lines with extra syllables, and other deviations from the expected ten-syllable line. If a line seems deviant, was Shakespeare sloppy? Is the text corrupt? Has the pronunciation changed? Or was he aiming for some dramatic effect?

Shakespeare did not leave us polished editions of his plays. But several hundred years of tinkering by scholars has provided the polishing and copy editing that Shakespeare failed to do. I have taken advantage of that scholarship and assume that any remaining anomalies are part of Shakespeare's design and must be respected. If the deviant meter is due to pronunciation change, then I find a metrical equivalent in contemporary English. If not, then the translation deviates in the same way as the original.

Of course no translation can perfectly capture both the sense and sound of poetry. When conflicts arise, I favor sense over strict adherence to the rhythm. Yet I do not allow a line to have a rhythm not found in Shakespeare's verse at the time he wrote the play.

For more information on Shakespeare's verse, see my translation of *Twelfth Night*. In that volume, "Appendix 1: How Iambic Pentameter Works" gives a detailed, accessible description of Shakespeare's iambic pentameter (available at www.FullMeasurePress.com).

About the Play

Shakespeare's *Romeo and Juliet*, the tragic story of two young lovers from feuding families who secretly marry, was most likely written and first performed around 1595. The play is Shakespeare's first attempt at tragedy using fictional rather than historical characters.

The story did not originate with Shakespeare but first appeared in Italian novellas in the late 15th century before making its way to England via a 3000-line verse rendering by Arthur Brooke in 1562 and a prose handling by William Painter in 1567. Shakespeare relied heavily on Brooke's version for the basic plot and incorporated some of his characterization, dialog, and imagery. But whereas Brooke's version is a longwinded, moralizing tale, Shakespeare's play is a masterpiece of tight plotting, vivid and concise characterization, rich and varied poetic experimentation, with surprisingly little hint of where Shakespeare's sympathies lie.

If you admire Shakespeare's later, more mature tragedies, you may be impatient with the unrelenting wordplay of the early scenes and the unnaturalness of the longish, somewhat lawyerly speeches, but don't let that keep you from noticing that Shakespeare had by this time become a master of character development. Every character, even minor ones, seems fully drawn and distinct, each equipped with strengths and weaknesses, capable of acting wisely or foolishly, convincing as they change colors right before our eyes.

Romeo, from the Montague clan, at first comes across as a comically love-sick youth, spouting Italian-style love poetry as he pines for a maiden so inaccessible that she never appears in the play. Later he comes alive before our eyes. He woos Juliet, the very real daughter of the rival Capulet family, takes on the amazing Mercutio in a battle of wits, loses control in a duel with Tybalt, reaffirms his love for Juliet, and contemplates suicide. He acts rashly when he meets Paris but then becomes deeply empathetic toward the unfortunate young man. Shakespeare makes these changes plausible. Juliet shows similar range. We see her first as a protected girl embarrassed by Nurse's frank, off-color discussion of the adolescent's future sex life. In less than a week, Juliet falls in love with a disturbing suddenness, secretly marries, sinks into despair, spends a night with her love, cuts all ties with her family, fakes a suicide, and wakes in a nightmarish setting. Such an intense compression of events seems improbable if we think about it much, yet Shakespeare makes it so believable that over 400 years later the names Romeo and Juliet still resonate and are household words even for people who have never read a line of Shakespeare.

As you read the play, give attention to Shakespeare's experiments with language and poetic style. The play's opening sonnet sets a formal, somber tone and gives away the ending. Then we meet two foolish, comic characters who trade too-obvious, grade-school sexual double-entendres before triggering a very serious brawl, broken up by the refined rhetoric of Prince Escalus. Romeo and his father appear separately, but both offer self-conscious examples of Renaissance-style versifying, laced with mythological references, elaborate personifications, and strained metaphors—all these events and styles in one scene. The play continues to shift between earthy dialog, flamboyant word-play, and highly formal, stylized rhetoric, but as Romeo and Juliet's plight and passion for each other become more desparate, their poetry becomes more original, beautiful, and heartfelt.

Juliet's language changes even more dramatically. We first see a tongue-tied adolescent who barely gets a word in. She blossoms when she meets Romeo, and the two trade lines of a sonnet that seem both studied and spontaneous. Her final extended soliloquy is a masterpiece of gothic horror as she contemplates waking in the family tomb next to the decomposing Tybalt not long after enjoying Romeo's warmth.

So where do Shakespeare's sympathies lie? Arthur Brooke's poem blames all parties. The Montagues and Capulets are mired in a pointless feud that leaves young people dead in the streets. Friar Lawrence grants absolution too quickly and comes up with a risky plan that turns disastrous with a single piece of bad luck. The nurse is a drunken gossip who allows young people to succumb to lust and marry secretly, reckless behavior that portrays the trust of her employers. And Romeo and Juliet are criticized for giving into lust and deceiving parents.

But Shakespeare complicates all this. Except perhaps for Tybalt, whose fiery hatred seems destructive and inexcusable, the other characters have sympathetic moments that only make their foolishness more frustrating. Juliet's Nurse, who abandons Juliet at her time of greatest vulnerability, has survived similar abandonment (loss of child and husband) and assumes Juliet can shrug this off. Friar Lawrence seems learned and sincere but opts for the same kind of rash action he cautions against. Even Capulet, who assumes his needs and hopes are shared by his daughter and auctions her off to the highest bidder as if she were a piece of livestock, shines at the masquerade party and shows kindness toward Romeo before behaving abominably when Juliet rejects his plans for her marriage to Paris. And to increase sympathy for the lovers, who do make dreadful decisions, Shakespeare makes them much too young—Juliet is only thirteen—to have the wisdom and patience to hold up under the weight of powerful emotions, foolish advice, family pressure, and clan warfare.

Some feel that Shakespeare allowed Fate, in the guise of a piece or two of bad luck, to play too big a part in the lovers' downfall. His later tragedies, they say, do not let characters off so easily. But Romeo and Juliet's world is one where foolishness rather than the naked ambition of a Macbeth or the wickedness of an Iago wreaks havoc. Shakespeare may be right to have luck play a role in a world where parents are no more responsible or patient than their children. Perhaps disaster is inevitable when passion, whether hate or love, rises so quickly and roams so freely.

Characters in the Play

Montague Household and Relatives
    MONTAGUE, Head of the Montague Household
    ROMEO, Son of Montague
    LADY MONTAGUE, Wife of Montague
    BALTHASAR, Servant of Romeo
    ABRAM, Servant of Montague
    BENVOLIO, Kinsman of the Montagues

Capulet Household and Relatives
    CAPULET, Head of the Capulet Household
    JULIET, Daughter of Capulet
    LADY CAPULET, Wife of Capulet
    NURSE to Juliet
    TYBALT, Kinsman of the Capulets
    SAMPSON, Servant of Capulet
    GREGORY, Servant of Capulet
    PETER, Servant of Juliet's Nurse
    CLOWN, **CHIEF SERVANT, ANTONY, POTPAN**, and
        other **SERVANTS** of Capulet
    An Old Man, **CAPULET'S COUSIN**

PRINCE ESCALUS, of Verona
MERCUTIO, Friend of Romeo, kinsman of Escalus
COUNTY PARIS, a young Nobleman, the Prince's Kinsman
PETRUCHIO, Friend of Tybalt
FRIAR LAWRENCE
FRIAR JOHN
An **HERBALIST**
Three **MUSICIANS**
Three **GUARDS**
CHORUS
Paris' **PAGE**; Tybalt's **PAGE,** Mercutio's **PAGE**
CITIZENS of Verona

Several men and women, servants, attendants, and relations to
both households; torchbearers, maskers.

Prologue

CHORUS
Two households, which in social standing match,
  In fair Verona, where we lay our scene,
Their ancient grudge is now a lawless clash,
  Where civil blood makes civil hands unclean.
Brought from the fatal loins of these two foes   5
  A pair of star-crossed lovers take their life;
And from their luckless fall compassion flows
  To bury with their death their parents' strife.
Their death-marked love pushed to its fearful end,
  And the persistence of their parents' rage,   10
Which nothing but their children's death could mend,
  Are now two hours of business on our stage;
And if you lend to us your patient ear,
What is not seen we strive to make appear.

Romeo and Juliet

Act One

Act One

Scene One. A Public Place

[Enter SAMPSON and GREGORY armed with
swords and bucklers (small shields)]

SAMPSON (servant of Capulet)
Gregory, I will not haul around the ashes my nose is rubbed
in.

GREGORY (servant of Capulet)
No, then we'd really be up to our ashes...collars in it.

SAMPSON
And if our choler's up, we'll draw our swords.

GREGORY
And when you die, you'll have a rope for a collar.   5

SAMPSON
I rise quickly when aroused.

GREGORY
But who would be quick to arouse you?

SAMPSON
A dog from the house of Montague aroused me.

GREGORY
To arouse is to move, but to be valiant is to stand firm. That's
why, if you are aroused, you just shrink away.   10

SAMPSON
A dog from that house has moved me to stand firm. I won't
give up my seat to any Montague man or woman.

GREGORY
That shows how weak a servant you are, for the weakest
is offered a seat.

SAMPSON
True, and that's why women, being the weaker vessels, are   15
always offered a seat. Therefore, I will knock Montague's
men off their seats and thrust his maidens onto mine.

GREGORY
The quarrel is between our masters and us men.

SAMPSON
One and the same. I'll show that I'm a tyrant. When I have
fought with the men, I will be humane to the maids; I will   20
cut off their heads.[1]

GREGORY
The heads of the maids?

SAMPSON
Yes, the heads of the maids, or their maidenheads. Take it
in whatever sense you wish.

GREGORY
They must take it in if they hope to sense it.   25

SAMPSON
Me they will sense as long as I remain firm, and it's well
known that I'm a pretty piece of flesh.

GREGORY
It's fortunate you are not a fish; if you were, you would be
a dried mackerel. Pull out your tool. Here are two from the
house of Montague.   30

[Enter two other servants, **ABRAM** and **BALTHASAR**]

SAMPSON
My naked weapon is out. Fight! I'll back you up.

GREGORY
What! By turning your back and running?

SAMPSON
No need to fear that.

GREGORY
I'm afraid I do fear that!

SAMPSON
Let's keep the law on our side. Let them start it.   35

GREGORY
I will sneer as I pass by, and let them take it as they
please.

SAMPSON
Or as they dare. I will suck my thumb toward them, which
will insult them if they notice it.

ABRAM (servant of Montague)
Are you flicking your thumb at us, sir?   40

SAMPSON
I am flicking my thumb, sir.

ABRAM
Are you flicking your thumb *at us*, sir?

SAMPSON
[To GREGORY] Is the law on our side if I say yes?

GREGORY
No.

SAMPSON
No, sir, I am not flicking my thumb at you, sir, but I *am*   45
flicking my thumb, sir.

GREGORY
Are you picking a fight, sir?

ABRAM
A fight, sir! No, sir.

SAMPSON
But if you are, sir, I'm ready for you. I serve as good a man
as you do.   50

ABRAM
But no better.

SAMPSON
Agreed, sir.

GREGORY
[to SAMPSON] Say "better." Here comes one of my master's
kinsmen. [seeing TYBALT coming at some distance]

SAMPSON
I mean, better, sir.   55

ABRAM
You lie.

SAMPSON
Draw, if you be men.—Gregory, remember your slashing
blow.

[They fight]
[Enter BENVOLIO]

BENVOLIO (kinsman of the Montagues)
Break it up, fools! Put down your swords. You know not
what you do.   60

[Beats down their swords]
[Enter TYBALT]

TYBALT (kinsman of the Capulets)
What, are you drawing on these spineless hens?
Turn now, Benvolio. Look upon your death.

BENVOLIO
I'm here to keep the peace. So sheathe your sword,
Or help me separate these men with it.

TYBALT
You draw yet talk of peace! I hate the word   65
As I hate hell, all Montagues, and you.
Take this, you coward!

[They fight]
[Enter several members of both houses, who join the fray;
then enter several CITIZENS with clubs and lances]

1ST CITIZEN (of Verona)
Clubs, pikes, and lances! Strike! And beat them down!
Down with the Capulets! Down with the Montagues!

[Enter CAPULET in his dressing
gown, and LADY CAPULET]

CAPULET (head of the Capulet Household)
What is this noise? Give me my long sword, ho!   70

LADY CAPULET (wife of Capulet)
A crutch, a crutch! What good's a sword to you?

CAPULET
My sword, I say! Old Montague has come,
And brandishes his blade to show his scorn.

[Enter MONTAGUE and LADY MONTAGUE,
who retrains MONTAGUE]

MONTAGUE (head of the Montague Household)
You villain Capulet!—[to his wife] Release me, let me go.

LADY MONTAGUE (wife of Montague)
You will not move one foot to seek a foe.   75

[Enter PRINCE ESCALUS, with ATTENDANTS]

PRINCE ESCALUS (of Verona)
Rebellious subjects, enemies of peace,
Profaning tools of peace with neighbors' blood—
Will they not listen? Hey! You men, you beasts,
Who quench the fire of your malicious rage
With crimson fountains springing from your veins—   80
On pain of torture, from your bloody hands
Throw your foul-tempered weapons to the ground
And hear the judgment of your outraged prince.
Three public brawls, sparked by a puff of breath,
From you, old Capulet, and Montague,   85
Have spoiled three-times the quiet of our streets
And made Verona's noblest citizens
Throw down the somber trappings of the wise
To wield in hands maligned by age and peace
A lance as old, to quell malignant hate.   90
If ever you disturb our streets again,
You'll pay for this disruption with your lives.
For now, the rest of you depart from here.
You, Capulet, will come along with me,
And, Montague, you'll come this afternoon,   95
To hear more of my ruling in this case,
To Freedom Hall, our public judgment-place.
Once more, on pain of death, all men depart.

[Exit PRINCE ESCALUS and ATTENDANTS;
CAPULET, LADY CAPULET, TYBALT, CITIZENS, and
SERVANTS]

MONTAGUE
Who opened up this ancient powder keg?
Speak, nephew. Were you here when it began?   100

BENVOLIO
Right there, the servants of your adversary
And yours were fighting hard when I arrived.
I drew to break it up, when instantly
The fiery Tybalt came, with drawn-out sword,
And as he breathed defiance in my ears,   105
He waved it all about and sliced the air,
But missing all, it hissed at him in scorn.
So there we fought, exchanging thrust for thrust
And blow for blow, one side against one side,
Until the prince made each side stand aside.   110

LADY MONTAGUE
O, where is Romeo? Was he here today?
Quite glad I am he was not in this fray.

BENVOLIO
Madam, an hour before the worshipped sun
Peered through the golden window of the east,
My troubled mind drove me to walk outside,   115
Where underneath the grove of sycamore
That grows along the city's western side,
I saw your son out on an early walk.
I moved towards him, but he detected me,
And slipped into the cover of the woods.   120
I, guessing his desires were much like mine—
To seek out most a place where few are found—
Explored my mood without exploring his,
And gladly dodged him when he gladly fled.

MONTAGUE
Many a morning people see him there,   125
His tears augmenting the fresh morning dew,
Adding to clouds more clouds with his deep sighs.
But then as soon as the cheer-giving sun
Draws back the shady curtains in the east
To wake Aurora, goddess of the dawn,   130
Avoiding light, my gloomy son slips home,
And pens himself up in his private room,

Puts up the shutters, locks dear daylight out
And gives himself an artificial night.
Ominous and black this mood will turn I'm sure,   135
Unless good guidance can produce a cure.

BENVOLIO
My noble uncle, do you know the cause?

MONTAGUE
No, I do not and can't find out a thing.

BENVOLIO
And have you tried to question him at all?

MONTAGUE
Yes, both myself and many other friends.   140
But since his feelings are his confidante,
He guides himself—how accurate I can't say—
And keeps himself so secret and closed up,
No one can take a reading of his state,
Just as the spiteful worm chews off the bud   145
Before it spreads its sweet leaves to the air
And offers up its beauty to the sun.[2]
If we can find out where his sorrows grow,
We'll give the cure the moment that we know.

BENVOLIO
Look, here he comes. So if you'll step aside,   150
I'll learn what's ailing him or know I've tried.

MONTAGUE
I hope you are rewarded for your stay
With true confession.—Come, madam, away.

[Exit MONTAGUE and LADY]
[Enter ROMEO]

BENVOLIO
Good morning, cousin.

ROMEO (son of Montague)
> Is the day that young?

BENVOLIO
It just struck nine.

ROMEO
> Poor me! Sad hours seem long.   155
Was that my father who went off so fast?

BENVOLIO
It was. What sadness lengthens Romeo's hours?

ROMEO
Not having that which, once had, makes them short.

BENVOLIO
In love?

ROMEO
Out.   160

BENVOLIO
Of love?

ROMEO
Out of her favor now that I'm in love.

BENVOLIO
Alas, that love, so gentle on first view,
In practice is so pitiless and cruel!

ROMEO
That love, whose view is hid behind a veil,   165
Without its eyes, can find desire's trail!
Where shall we eat?—O my! Who battled here?
Yet never mind, for I have heard it all.
With hate there's much to-do, but more with love.[3]
Why, then, this wrangling love! This loving hate!   170
O anything, since nothing can create!

Then heavy lightness, serious foolishness!
A chaos fashioned from well-structured forms!
Feathers of lead, clear smoke, cold fire, sick health!
A wakeful sleep that's never what it is!   175
This love I feel, I feel no love for this.
You do not laugh?

BENVOLIO
                    No, coz, I'd rather weep.

ROMEO
At what, good heart?

BENVOLIO
                    At your good heart's oppression.

ROMEO
But that is love's transgression.
Grief all my own lies heavy in my breast,   180
Which you'll increase if I become depressed
By some of yours. This love that you have shown
Will add more grief to those that are my own.
Love is a smoke raised from the fumes of sighs,
If cleared, a fire that sparks in lovers' eyes;   185
If riled, a sea that's fed with lovers' tears.
What else is it? A madness most astute,
A sweet preserved in dirt and bitter fruit.
Farewell, my coz. [Going]

BENVOLIO
                    Slow down! I'll come along.
If you just leave like this, you do me wrong.   190

ROMEO
Tut! I have lost myself, I am not here.
This is not Romeo. He is off somewhere.

BENVOLIO
Be serious now. Who is it that you love?

ROMEO
Be somber when I tell you?

BENVOLIO
                Somber? No.
Be serious, tell me who.   195

ROMEO
A man with serious sickness makes his will—
A word ill-chosen for a man so ill!
Quite seriously, coz, I love a woman.

BENVOLIO
My aim was good when I guessed it was love.

ROMEO
A perfect shot!—She stands out from the rest.   200

BENVOLIO
A target that stands out is easily hit.

ROMEO
You missed the mark. This goddess takes no hits
From Cupid's bow—she has Diana's wits.
With battle-tested chastity well armed,
Love's weak and childish bow leaves her uncharmed.   205
She will not be besieged by words of love,
Or seek engagement with assailing eyes,
Or bathe herself with saint-seducing gold.
She's rich in beauty now, and only poor
If beauty dies with her when she's no more.   210

BENVOLIO
Then she has promised always to be chaste?

ROMEO
She has, but saving it just swells the waste;
For beauty, slain by her severity,
Cuts beauty off from all posterity.
She is too fair, too wise, wisely too fair,   215

She saves her soul by making me despair.
She has renounced all love, and with that vow
He who lives dead must live to tell it now.

BENVOLIO
Take my advice, forget, don't think of her.

ROMEO
O, teach me how I can forget to think.   220

BENVOLIO
By granting liberty to both your eyes.
Examine other beauties.

ROMEO
                              That's a way
To dwell upon her excellence all the more.
Because these masks that shade these lovely brows
Are black, our minds assume their skin is pale.   225
He who is struck with blindness can't forget
The precious treasure of the eyesight lost.
Show me a girl with beauty unsurpassed;
What good's her beauty if it's just a note
I read to know she's passed the unsurpassed?   230
Farewell. You cannot teach me to forget.

BENVOLIO
I'll pay for lessons till I die in debt.

[Exit]

Scene Two. A Street in Verona

[Enter CAPULET, COUNTY PARIS, and CLOWN]

CAPULET
But Montague's been warned as much as I,

The penalty's the same, and it's not hard, I think,
For men so old as we to keep the peace.

COUNTY PARIS (a young nobleman)
By my appraisal, you're of equal worth,
A pity that you've lived at odds so long.   5
But now my lord, about what I've proposed.

CAPULET
I'll say again what I have said before.
My child is still a novice in this world.
She has not seen her fourteenth year pass by.
The glory of two summers should subside   10
Before we judge her ripe to be a bride.

COUNTY PARIS
From younger ones are happy mothers bred.

CAPULET
And marred too soon when they're so quickly wed.
Earth has swallowed all my other hopes—
She's my only hope left on this earth⁴   15
But woo her, noble Paris, win her heart;
The choice is hers, my will is but one part.
My plans must stay within her range of choice
Then we'll agree with one assenting voice.
Tonight I have invited friends of old,   20
To join a long-established feast I hold.
Just ones I love, and you are one of those,
One more's quite welcome, and the number grows.
At my poor house you will behold tonight
Earth-dancing stars that make dark heaven light.   25
Those pleasures that each robust young man feels
When green-clad April dances on the heels
Of limping winter— even that delight
Comes with fresh fragrant buds that you tonight
Inherit at my house. Hear all, come see,   30
And like her most whose worth adds up to be
The highest of them all, for mine's just one
And (since one's not "a number") counts as none.⁵

Come, go with me. [to the CLOWN] Boy, gallop all about
Through fair Verona, seeking all those out   35
Whose names are listed here, [hands him a paper] and to
  them say,
My house awaits the pleasure of their stay.

[Exit CAPULET and COUNTY PARIS]

CLOWN (servant of Capulet)
Seek out whoever's listed here! It may as well say that the
shoemaker will be fiddling with his meat and the butcher
with his leather, the painter with his rod, and the fisherman   40
with his brush. I am sent to find the people whose names
are written here yet have no way of knowing what the writer
wrote. I must find a scholar. Help's arrived!

[Enter BENVOLIO and ROMEO]

BENVOLIO
Tut, man, as one fire dies, the next's beginning;
  New pains arrive as soon as old ones languish.   45
Forward you're dizzy, then try backward spinning.
  Unceasing grief is cured by a new anguish.
Contract some new infection in your eye,
The virulence of the old one soon will die.

ROMEO
I'm sure your cure-all's excellent for that.   50

BENVOLIO
For what if I may ask?

ROMEO
                            A knee that's skinned.

BENVOLIO
Why, Romeo, are you mad?

ROMEO
Not mad, but strapped down more than madmen are,

Shut up in prison, kept there with no food,
With whippings, torture and—Good day, good fellow.   55

CLOWN
Good evening, sir.—Please tell me, can you read?

ROMEO
Yes, my own fortune in my misery.

CLOWN
Perhaps that could be learned by heart. But tell me, can
you read all that you see?

ROMEO
Yes, if I know the letters and the language.   60

CLOWN
An honest answer. Take care! [starts to leave]

ROMEO
Wait, fellow. I can read. [Reads]
  "Signior Martino and his wife and daughters; County
  Anselmo and his gorgeous sisters; the lady widow
  of Vitruvio; Signior Placentio and his lovely nieces;   65
  Mercutio and his brother Valentine; my uncle Capulet,
  his wife, and daughters; my fair niece Rosaline; Livia;
  Signior Valentio and his cousin Tybalt; Lucio and the
  lively Helena."
A sizable assembly. [Gives back the paper] And go where?   70

CLOWN
On over.

ROMEO
And where? To supper?

CLOWN
To our house.

ROMEO
Whose house?

CLOWN
My master's.   75

ROMEO
No doubt I should have asked you that before.

CLOWN
Now I'll tell you without you asking. My master is the
great rich Capulet, and if you're not from the house of
Montague, please come on over and down a cup of wine.
Take care!   80

[Exit]

BENVOLIO
At this perennial feast of Capulet's
Fair Rosaline whom you so love will dine
With all the stunning beauties of Verona.
Go there, and with your uninfected eye,
Compare her face with others I will show,   85
And I will make you think your swan's a crow.

ROMEO
If this devout religion in my eyes
   Maintained such falsehood, tears would turn to fire;
These heretics, though often dunked, would rise
   And once seen through, would then be burnt as liars!   90
One finer than my love? The all-seeing sun,
Since time began, knows she is matched by none.

BENVOLIO
You'll think she's fine till someone else walks by,
She's gauged against herself in either eye;
So since your crystal scales have not yet weighed   95
Your ladylove against some other maid
I'll show you who is shining at this feast,
And she, who now seems best, may seem the least.

ROMEO
I'll go along, not to be shown such sights,
But to rejoice in my love's sparkling lights.   100

[Exit]

Scene Three. A Room in Capulet's House

[Enter LADY CAPULET and NURSE]

LADY CAPULET
Nurse, where's my daughter? Call her in to me.

NURSE (to Juliet)
I swear upon the twelve years I was chaste,
I've asked her to.—Hey, lamb! Hey, ladybird!
God forbid! Where's that girl? Hey, Juliet!

[Enter JULIET]

JULIET (daughter of Capulet)
Who's calling me?   5

NURSE
Your mother.

JULIET
Madam, I am here. What is it you wish?

LADY CAPULET
There is this matter.—Nurse, give us a minute,
We must talk privately.—Nurse, come back in.
On second thought, you should be part of this.   10
You know my daughter's reached a tender age.

NURSE
Indeed, I know her age down to the hour.

LADY CAPULET
She's not fourteen.

NURSE
I'll tender fourteen of my teeth—and yet, let it be said my
tender gums now hold just four—that she is not fourteen.   15
How long is it to the harvest festival?

LADY CAPULET
Two weeks and a few odd days.

NURSE
Even or odd, of all days in the year,
The night before that day she'll turn fourteen.
Susan and she—God rest all Christian souls!—   20
Ages the same. Well, Susan is with God;
She was too good for me. But, as I said,
The night before that day she'll be fourteen.
By god she will. And I remember it well.
The earthquake was eleven years ago,   25
And she was weaned—I never will forget it—
Of all the days that year, upon that day,
For I had just spread mustard on my dug,
Sitting in the sun near the pigeon coop.
My lord and you were then at Mantua—   30
Yes, I do have a brain—well, as I said,
Just when she tasted mustard on my nipple
And felt it sting, to see the pretty fool
Make such a fuss and fall out with my dug!
"I'm shaking," said the coop. No need, I swear,   35
To tell me to skedaddle.
And since that time it's been eleven years.
By then, God knows, she's standing on her own,
And could have run and waddled all about,
For just the day before, she bumped her head.   40
And then my husband—God be with his soul,
A merry man he was—picked up the child.
"Oh my," said he, "did you fall on your face?
You'll fall face up, knees out once you know more,
Will you not, Jule?" and, by the holy dame,   45

The pretty wretch quit crying, "Yes", says she.
And now to think that jest will come about!
I tell you, if I live a thousand years,
I never will forget it. "Will you not, Jule?" says he.
The pretty fool, stops cold, and "Yes", says she.   50

LADY CAPULET
Enough of this. Could you please hold your peace?

NURSE
Yes, madam, yet I cannot help but laugh,
To think her crying stopped and "Yes," says she.
And yet, I tell you, on her forehead was
A bump as big as a young rooster's ball,   55
A perilous knock, and she cried bitterly.
"Oh," says my husband, "fell down on your face?
You'll fall face up soon as you come of age,
Will you not, Jule?" Stops cold, and "Yes," says she.

JULIET
I'll stop you cold, I tell you, "Yes," says I.   60

NURSE
I'm through. And may you be among the chosen!
You were the prettiest babe I ever nursed.
If I could live to see you wed someday,
I'd have my wish.

LADY CAPULET
Such merry talk, when marrying's the thing   65
I wish to speak of.—Tell me, daughter Juliet,
What inclinations do you have toward marriage?

JULIET
Of such an honor I have never dreamed.

NURSE
An honor! Were I not your only nurse,
I'd say you'd sucked some wisdom from some teat.   70

LADY CAPULET
Start thinking of it. Younger ones than you,
Here in Verona, ladies of esteem,
Are having children. By my reckoning,
I was a mother at about your age
And you're not even married. Here's my point: 75
The valiant Paris seeks your hand in marriage.

NURSE
A man, young lady! Why there's no such man
In all the world—and carved from wax he is.

LADY CAPULET
Verona's summer does not have such flowers.

NURSE
Yes, he's a flower, indeed, a flower for sure.   80

LADY CAPULET
Say something. Can you love this gentleman?
Tonight you will observe him at our feast.
Read through the pages of the young man's face,
Where beauty's pen has written down delight.
Examine close the marriage of each line,   85
And see the harmony lent by its design.
Whatever this fine volume may disguise
It's written in the margin of his eyes.
This precious book of love, this unbound lover,
To reach full beauty only needs a cover.   90
The fish lives in the sea, and there's much pride
When beauty hid within can show outside.
A binding in most eyes will share the glory,
When gold clasps lock within a golden story.
And you will share all that he may possess,   95
By having him, you make yourself no less.

NURSE
No less? No, bigger. Men make women swell.

LADY CAPULET
Be to the point. Is Paris to your liking?

JULIET
I'm looking to like him, if looks prompt liking.
But darts will only shoot out of my eye   100
As far as your approval makes them fly.

[Enter a SERVANT]

SERVANT
Madam, the guests are here, supper's being served, you're
being called, my young lady's being asked for, the nurse
is being cursed in the kitchen, and everything is urgent. I
must go serve them. I beg you, come at once.   105

LADY CAPULET
We'll follow you.

[Exit SERVANT]

Juliet, the county's waiting.

NURSE
Go, girl, add happy nights to happy days.

[Exit]

Scene Four. A Street Outside the Capulet's Party

[Enter ROMEO, MERCUTIO, BENVOLIO, with five or
six maskers, several torch-bearers, and others]

ROMEO
Should I explain our presence with a speech?
Or just approach without apology?

BENVOLIO
Verbosity of that sort's out-of-date.
No Cupid please, his blindfold's just some scarf,
His lip-shaped bow mere painted slats of wood,   5
Scaring the ladies like a scarecrow might,
No fumbling prologue, half from memory,
Half from my prompting, stating we've arrived.
Let them take measure of us as they choose,
We'll tap them out a measure, and be gone.   10

ROMEO
Hand me a torch. I'm in no mood for strutting.
Weighed down by sadness, I will bear the light.

MERCUTIO (friend of Romeo, kinsman of Escalus)
No, gentle Romeo, we must have you dance.

ROMEO
Not I, believe me. You have dancing shoes
With nimble soles. I have a soul of lead   15
Staked to the ground so firmly I can't move.

MERCUTIO
You are in love, so borrow Cupid's wings,
And soar with them above the common bounds.

ROMEO
I'm much too sore from his deep-piercing shaft
To soar with his light feathers, and so bound   20
I cannot bound one notch above deep woe.
Beneath the heavy weight of love I've sunk.

MERCUTIO
Sink into it and love will feel your weight,
Too great a load for such a tender thing.

ROMEO
Is love a tender thing? It is too rough,   25
Too rude, too boisterous, and it pricks like thorns.

MERCUTIO
If love's been rough with you, be rough with love.
Just prick it back and you can beat love down.—
Give me a mask to put my face inside.— [Puts on a mask]
Disguising a disguise! And so who cares   30
If curious eyes make note of some defect?
These beetle-brows can do my blushing for me.

BENVOLIO
Come, knock and enter, but once we are in,
Then every man had best take to his heels.

ROMEO
The torch. [takes the torch] Let pleasure-seekers, light of
     heart,   35
Arouse unfeeling sawdust with their heels,
For I'm the subject of this grand old saying:
The candle-holder wins yet does not play.
If I sit still, the game may come my way.[6]

MERCUTIO
Still as a mouse, as useless as the sheriff.   40
And you sit still because you're mired in piles
Of—mind my tongue—of love, and stuck in it
Up to your ears. Let's go, we're burning daylight.

ROMEO
No, that's not so.

MERCUTIO
                    I mean, with this delay
We're wasting light, like lighting lights by day.   45
Head straight for what I mean, for common sense
Runs five time faster than intelligence.[7]

ROMEO
We do mean well in going to this masque,
But there's no sense in going.

MERCUTIO
                              Why, may I ask?

ROMEO
I dreamt a dream last night.

MERCUTIO
                And so did I.   50
ROMEO
Well, what was yours?

MERCUTIO
                That dreamers often lie.
ROMEO
In bed asleep, while things they dream are true.

MERCUTIO
O, then, I see Queen Mab has been with you,
The midwife of the fairies, and she comes
No bigger than the carvings on a ring   55
On the fore-finger of an alderman,
Drawn by a team of little miniatures
Across men's noses as they lie asleep.
Her wagon-spokes are made of spider legs;
The cover, of the wings of grasshoppers;   60
The harness, of the smallest spinner's web;
The collars, of the moonlight's watery beams;
Her whip, of cricket bones; the lash, of thread;
Her wagoneer, a small gray-coated gnat,
Not half as big as some round little mite   65
Pricked from the eyebrow of a lazy maid.
Her chariot's an empty hazel-nut,
Chiseled by squirrels and bored out by old grubs,
The fairies' coachmakers, since time began.
She gallops in such splendor night by night   70
Through lovers' brains, and then they dream of love;
Past courtiers' knees, who then will dream of bowing,
Past lawyers' fingers, who then dream of fees;
Past ladies' lips, who dream of being kissed,
Which angry Mab will often plague with sores,   75
Because their breath's polluted by sweet treats.
Sometimes she gallops past that courtier's nose,
And dreams he gets to press his patron's suit.

And sometimes with a pig's tail she will come,
Tickling a parson's nose when he's asleep,   80
And then he dreams he gets a different post.
Sometimes she rides above a soldier's neck,
And then he dreams of cutting foreign throats,
Of ambushes, breached walls, and Spanish blades,
Of drinks he quaffs five gallons deep, but soon   85
Drums in his ear will make him flinch and wake,
And, terrified, he says a prayer or two,
And sleeps again. This is the same queen Mab
Who snarls the manes of horses in the night,
And twists the knots in foul and sluttish hair—   90
Untangle it and much misfortune bodes—
A nightmare who, when maids lie on their backs,
Lays weight on them, to show them how to bear
The load that makes them women of good carriage.
This is she...

ROMEO
　　　　　　　Peace, peace, Mercutio, peace,   95
Your talk is empty.

MERCUTIO
　　　　　　　True, I talk of dreams,
Which are the children of an idle brain,
Begot from nothing but some empty whims,
Which are as thin in substance as the air,
And more inconstant than the wind, which woos   100
Just now the frozen bosom of the north,
But, angered, turns and puffs a different way,
Turning to drop its dew upon the south.

BENVOLIO
This wind you talk of carries us away.
Supper is done, and we'll arrive too late.   105

ROMEO
Too early, I'm afraid. My mind can sense
Some fearful mortgage, hanging in the stars,
That, with these revels, bitterly begins,

Events to come in which the terms expire
Of this detested life held in my breast,   110
Vile forfeiture, its cause untimely death.
Let he who has the helm that steers my course
Direct my sails!⁸ On, lusty gentlemen!

BENVOLIO
Strike, drummer.

[Exit]

Scene Five. A Hall in Capulet's House

[MUSICIANS waiting. Enter SERVANTS]

CHIEF SERVANT (of CAPULET)
Potpan leaves just when the cleanup starts. Him remove a
platter? Him scrape off a platter?

2ⁿᵈ SERVANT
When the only helping hands are too busy to be washed,
it's a foul thing.

CHIEF SERVANT
Fold up the chairs, put away the sideboard, take care of the   5
silverware.—Be good, save me a piece of marzipan, and do
me a favor, tell the porter to let in Susan Grindstone and
Nell. Antony and Potpan!

[Enter ANTONY and POTPAN]

ANTONY (servant of Capulet)
Yes, ready.

CHIEF SERVANT
You're being looked for and called for, asked for and hunted   10
for in the great chamber.

POTPAN (servant of Capulet)
We cannot be here and there too.—Be cheerful, boys! Be
quick about it, and the last alive takes all.

[SERVANTS exit towards the rear]
[Enter CAPULET and his household, SERVANTS, maskers and accompanying women, ROMEO, MERCUTIO,
and BENVOLIO]

CAPULET
Welcome, gentlemen! Ladies who have toes
Unplagued by corns will dance a turn with you.—   15
Ah, my fine ladies! And which one of you
Will now decline to dance? The one who's coy,
I'll say her corns hurt. Have I hit a nerve?
Welcome, gentlemen! There was once a time
When I'd have worn a mask and could have told   20
A whispered tale in a fair lady's ear
That would have pleased her. But, it's gone, gone, gone.
You are welcome, gentlemen! Come, musicians, play.
[to the SERVANTS] The floor—the floor!—Make room!
    Girls, move your feet.

[Music plays, and they dance]

More light, you knaves, and fold the tables up,   25
And quench the fire, the room has grown too hot.—
[greeting a guest] Welcome, my boy, an unexpected joy.
[to CAPULET'S COUSIN] No, sit. No, sit, good cousin
    Capulet,
For you and I are past our dancing days.
How long now has it been since you and I   30
Have worn a mask?

CAPULET'S COUSIN (an old man)
                It must be thirty years.

CAPULET
What, man! It's not that long, it's not that long.

It's since the wedding of Lucentio,
This coming August, coming soon in fact,
Some five and twenty years; we've masked since then.   35

CAPULET'S COUSIN
It's more, it's more. His son is older, sir;
His son is thirty.

CAPULET
          No, that can't be right.
Two years ago, his son was still a teen.

ROMEO
[to a SERVANT] That lady there, enriching that
   knight's hand,
Who is she?   40

SERVANT
I do not know, sir.

ROMEO
O, she could teach the torches to burn bright!
It seems she's hanging from the cheek of night
Like a rich jewel in a chieftain's ear—
Beauty too rich for use, for earth too dear!   45
And seems a snowy dove lined up with crows,
Among her friends, that's how the lady shows.
The dance now done, I'll note where she will rest
And, touching hers, my rough hands will be blessed.
Has my heart loved till now? Renounce past sight!   50
I've never seen true beauty till this night.

TYBALT
This, by his voice, must be a Montague.—
Fetch me my rapier, boy. How dare this slave
Come in here covered with a comic face,
To mock and sneer at our festivities!   55
Now, by the worthy lineage of my kin,
To strike him dead cannot be held a sin.

CAPULET
Now, tell me, kinsman why you fume like this?

TYBALT
Uncle, this is a Montague, our foe,
A lowlife, who has come here out of spite,   60
To sneer at our festivities tonight.

CAPULET
Young Romeo, is it?

TYBALT
                    It is, that lowlife, Romeo.

CAPULET
Compose yourself, dear cousin, let him be.
He has the conduct of a gentleman,
And I hear all Verona brags of him   65
As being a virtuous, well-mannered youth.
For all the wealth that's in this town I won't
Here in my house be impolite to him.
Therefore be calm and take no note of him.
That is my wish, which surely you respect,   70
So put a good face on, take off these frowns,
An unbecoming image for a feast.

TYBALT
It fits, when such a lowlife is a guest,
I won't endure him.

CAPULET
                    He shall be endured.
You, farmer boy, I say he shall. Enough.   75
Am I the master here, or you? Enough.
You won't endure him! May God save my soul,
You'll start a ruckus here among my guests!
You'll cause a free-for-all! You'll be the boss!

TYBALT
But, uncle, it's a slap.

CAPULET

                     Enough, enough!   80
You childish yokel.—[to others] Is that so, indeed?—
[to TYBALT] This foolishness may wound you. Now I see:
You dare to cross me! Now the time has come—
[to the DANCERS] Well done, you dears!—[to TYBALT]
    You prancing rooster, go.
Be quiet, or—[to the SERVANTS] More light, more
    light!—Come now!   85
[to TYBALT] I'll quiet you. [to the DANCERS] Yes!—
    Briskly now, you dears.

TYBALT

Enforced restraint and stubborn anger meeting
Makes my flesh tremble at the two competing.
I will withdraw: but this intrusion will
Soon make what seems so sweet a bitter pill.   90

                [Exit]

ROMEO

[To JULIET] If I profane with my unworthy hand
  This holy shrine, my gentle sin is this:
My lips, two blushing pilgrims, here they stand
  To smooth that rough touch with a tender kiss.

JULIET

Good pilgrim, you have wronged your hand too much, 95
  I see a fitting piety in this;
For saints have hands that pilgrims' hands may touch,
  And palm to palm is how the holy kiss.

ROMEO

Don't saints have lips, and holy pilgrims too?

JULIET

Yes, pilgrim, lips that they must use in prayer.   100

ROMEO

O, then, dear saint, let lips do what hands do;
They pray, saints act, or faith turns to despair.

JULIET
Saints won't move first, though prayers may make them
act.

ROMEO
Then do not move as my prayer takes effect.

[He kisses her]

Thus from my lips, by yours, my sin is purged.   105

JULIET
Then from my lips take back the sin they took.

ROMEO
Sin from my lips? A wrong so sweetly urged!
Give back my sin.

[He kisses her]

JULIET
                    I see you've read the book.

NURSE
Madam, your mother begs a word with you.

ROMEO
Who is her mother?

NURSE
                    Heaven's sake, young man,   110
Her mother is the lady of the house.
And a good lady, and she's wise and virtuous.
I nursed her daughter who you're talking with.
I tell you, he who can grab hold of her
Will get the cash.

ROMEO
                    Is she a Capulet?   115
A costly deal! My life's owed to a foe.

BENVOLIO
Come on, let's leave. We'll quit while we're ahead.

ROMEO
Yes, more means more unrest, and that I dread.

CAPULET
No, gentlemen, don't think of leaving yet.
A modest, light refreshment's coming up.—   120

[The guests gesture that they must leave]

If you insist? Why then, I thank you all.
I thank you, honest gentlemen. Good-night.—
[to the SERVANTS] More torches here! [to help the
    guests out]—Come on then, time for bed.
Yes, fellow, that is true, it's growing late.   125
It's time to rest.

[Exit all but JULIET and NURSE]

JULIET
Please come here, nurse. Who is that gentleman?

NURSE
The son and heir of old Tiberio.

JULIET
Who is the one now going out the door?

NURSE
If I'm not wrong, that's young Petruchio.   130

JULIET
And who's that one, the one that would not dance?

NURSE
I don't know.

JULIET
Go ask his name. If he's already wed,
My grave will likely be my wedding-bed.

NURSE
His name is Romeo, and a Montague,   135
The only son of your great enemy.

JULIET
My only love sprung from my only hate!
And seen before I knew, now known too late!
An ominous birth of love it is to me,
That I must love and loathe an enemy.   140

NURSE
What's this? What's this?

JULIET
                    A rhyme I learned just now
From one with whom I danced.

              [A voice calls from within, "Juliet."]

NURSE
                    Come on, Come on!
Come, let's go in. The guests are now all gone.

                    [Exit]

Romeo and Juliet

Act Two

Act Two

[Enter CHORUS]

CHORUS
While in his deathbed old desire now lies,
  And young affection yearns to be his heir.
The loveliness for which love groans and dies,
  With tender Juliet now cannot compare.
Now he's in love and she with Romeo,   5
  The two of them bewitched and charmed by looks,
But he begs favors from a so-called foe,
  While she steals love's sweet bait from fearful hooks.
Since he's a foe, he lacks an avenue
  To breathe the vows that lovers tend to swear,   10
Though she's as much in love, her means are few
  To meet her new belovéd anywhere.
But passion lends them strength and time to meet,
Intensity that turns intensely sweet.

[Exit]

Scene One. Outside Capulet's Garden Wall

[Enter ROMEO]

ROMEO
Can I depart when now my heart is here?
Turn back, dead earth, and sink back to your core.

[ROMEO turns back, withdrawing]

57

[Enter BENVOLIO and MERCUTIO]

BENVOLIO
Romeo! My cousin Romeo!

MERCUTIO
                        Fooled again;
As sure as life, he's slipped off home to bed.

BENVOLIO
He ran this way and hopped this orchard wall.   5
Call him, Mercutio.

MERCUTIO
                        No, I'll conjure him.
[indicates a conjuring circle] Romeo! Juices! Madman!
    Passion! Lover!
Appear now in the likeness of a sigh.
Speak just one rhyme, and I am satisfied.
Cry out "Poor me!" Just utter "Love" and "Dove".   10
Speak to my buddy Venus one kind word,
One nickname for her sightless son and heir,
Young Cupid, Senior, he who shot so true[1]
And forced some king to wed a beggar-maid.—
He doesn't hear, he doesn't wake, he doesn't move.   15
Our pup plays dead, so I must conjure him.—
I conjure you with Rosaline's bright eyes,
With her high forehead and her scarlet lip,
With her fine foot, straight leg, and swaying thigh,
And those domains that lie there so close by,   20
So that your likeness will appear to us!

BENVOLIO
But if he hears you, you will anger him.

MERCUTIO
This cannot anger him. 'Twould anger him
To raise a spirit in her magic circle,
Draw out its essence, letting it stand there   25

Till she extracts its charm, and casts it down.
Yes, that would hurt. My incantation now
Is fair and honest. In his lady's name,
I only conjure him to make him rise.

BENVOLIO
Come, he has hid himself among these trees,   30
To seek the company of this soggy night.
Blind is his love, best suited to the dark.

MERCUTIO
If love is blind, love cannot hit the mark.
Now he will sit beneath a tree of figs,
And wish his mistress were the kind of fruit   35
That maidens laugh about when they're alone.
O Romeo, if she were, O if she were
A ripened fig and you a rhubarb stalk.
Romeo, good night.—My trundle bed awaits;
This open ground's too cold for me to sleep.—   40
Come, shall we go?

BENVOLIO
                    Let's do. It makes no sense
To seek one who does not wish to be found.

[Exit]

Scene Two. Capulet's Garden

[Enter ROMEO]

ROMEO
So mock my scars—you've never felt a wound.

[JULIET appears above at a window]

But wait! What light dawns through the window there?

It is the east, and Juliet is the sun!
Arise, fair sun, and kill the envious moon,
Whose goddess is now sick and pale with grief,   5
Since her devoted maid's more fair than she.
Do not remain her maid—she's envious.
Her chaste attire's anemic, sickly green,
And only jesters wear it. Cast it off.
It is my lady. O, it is my love!   10
O, if she knew she were!—[pauses]
She speaks, yet she says nothing. What is this?
Her eye's conversing, I will answer it.
I am too bold, it's not to me she speaks.
Two of the fairest stars in all the heavens,   15
Off on some errand now, have asked her eyes
To twinkle in their place till they return.
What if her eyes were stars, and stars her eyes?
The brightness of her cheek would shame those stars,
As daylight does a lamp. Her eyes in heaven   20
Would through that airy region gleam so bright
That birds would sing and not know it was night.
See how she leans her cheek against her hand!
If I could be a glove upon that hand,
Then I might touch that cheek!

JULIET

                Ah me!

ROMEO

                       She speaks.   25
O, speak again, bright angel, for you are
As glorious to the night that's overhead
As is a soaring messenger from heaven
On whom the white and upward wondering eyes
Of mortal souls roll back to fix their gaze   30
When he hops on the lazy, passing clouds[2]
And sails upon the bosom of the air.

JULIET
O Romeo, Romeo! Why must you be Romeo?

Disown your father and reject your name.
Or, if you won't, then swear to me your love,   35
And I'll no longer be a Capulet.

ROMEO

[Aside] Should I hear more, or should I answer this?

JULIET

It's just your name that is my enemy.
You are yourself, and not a Montague.
What's Montague? It's neither hand, nor foot,   40
Nor arm, nor face, nor any other part
Belonging to a man. O, be some other name!
What's in a name? That thing we call a rose
By any other name would smell as sweet.
And Romeo would, if Romeo weren't his name,   45
Retain the dear perfection that he holds
Without that label. Romeo, shed your name,
And trade that word, which is not part of you,
For all of me.

ROMEO

        I'll take you at your word.
Just call me love and christen me again.   50
From now on I will not be Romeo.

JULIET

What man is this behind the screen of night,
Who's stumbled on my thoughts?

ROMEO

             With just a name
I don't know how to tell you who I am.
My name, dear saint, is hateful to myself,   55
Because it is an enemy to you.
Were I to write it, I'd tear up that word.

JULIET

My ears have still not drunk a hundred words

Poured from that tongue, and yet I know the sound.
Are you not Romeo, and a Montague?   60

ROMEO
Neither, fair saint, if you're displeased by them.

JULIET
How did you get here? Tell me how and why?
The orchard walls are high and hard to climb,
A deadly place, considering who you are,
If any of my kinsmen find you here.   65

ROMEO
With love's light wings, I overcame these walls,
For stony barriers cannot keep love out.
Whatever love can do, love will attempt,
And so your kinsmen cannot hinder me.

JULIET
But if they see you, they will murder you.   70

ROMEO
Alas, more peril lies there in your eye
Than twenty of their swords. Just one sweet look,
And I am shielded from their enmity.

JULIET
For all the world they must not see you here.

ROMEO
This cloak of night will hide me from their sight;   75
If you don't love me, let them find me here.
I'd rather have their hatred end my life
Than live, my death postponed, without your love.

JULIET
And whose directions helped you find this place?

ROMEO
Why, love himself first pushed me to inquire.   80

He lent advice, and I lent him my eyes.
I can't read charts, but if you washed away
To some vast shore across the farthest sea,
I'd venture there to gain such merchandise.

JULIET
You know the mask of night is on my face,   85
Or else a maiden's blush would paint my cheeks
All due to what you heard me say to-night.
I'd gladly stick to form, yes, yes deny
What I have said. But farewell etiquette!
Do you love me? I know you will say yes.   90
Your word's enough. But if you swear it's so,
You then may prove untrue. They say Jove laughs
At lovers' tricks. O gentle Romeo,
If you're in love, give all your faith to me.
Or if you think that I'm too easily won,   95
I'll frown, turn cold to love, and tell you no,
For no good reason but to make you woo.
In truth, fair Montague, I'm too in love,
And you may think I lightly do such things.
But trust me, gentle man, I'll prove more true   100
Than those who act reserved to catch your eye.
I should be more reserved, I must confess,
But then you overheard, unknown to me,
The passion of my love. Forgive me then—
A love's not light because it yields so soon,   105
And that's a truth this dark night has divulged.

ROMEO
Lady, I swear upon the blessèd moon
That tints with silver all these fruit-tree tops—

JULIET
O, don't swear by the moon, inconstant moon,
Whose circular orb will change from day to day,   110
Or else your love will be as variable.

ROMEO
Then what should I swear to?

JULIET
>   Don't swear at all.
Or swear to you, yourself, a state so graced,
That it's the god of my idolatry,
And I'll believe you.

ROMEO
>   If my heart's dear love—   115

JULIET
No, do not swear. Though overjoyed with you,
I feel no joy in trading vows tonight.
It is too rash, too ill-considered, sudden,
Too much like lightning, which before one says
The word has ceased to be. My sweet, good night!   120
This bud of love may bloom with summer's breath
And prove a gorgeous flower when we next meet.
Good night, good night! May sweet repose and rest
Come to your heart as they have in my breast!

ROMEO
O, will you leave me so unsatisfied?   125

JULIET
What satisfaction can you gain tonight?

ROMEO
Exchange your vow of faithful love for mine.

JULIET
I gave you mine before you even asked,
Yet wish I had it back to give again.

ROMEO
You would withdraw it? For what purpose, love?   130

JULIET
To burst with it and give it once again.
And yet I only wish for what I have.
My bounty is as boundless as the sea,

My love as deep. The more I give to thee,
The more I have, for both are infinite.   135
I hear a noise within. Dear love, adieu!—

[NURSE calls from within]

Hold on, good nurse!—Sweet Montague, be true.
Stay here a moment; I will come again.

[Exit]

ROMEO
O blessèd, blessèd night! I am afraid,
This being night, all this is just a dream,   140
Deception far too sweet to be for real.

[Enter JULIET above]

JULIET
Three words, dear Romeo, and good night indeed.
If honorable intentions guide your love,
Your purpose marriage, send me word tomorrow,
Through someone I'll arrange to come to you,   145
On where and at what time you'll make your pledge,
And I'll lay all my fortunes at your feet
And follow you, my lord, throughout the world.

NURSE
[From within] Madam!

JULIET
I'm coming, nurse.—But if you don't mean well,   150
I will insist that—

NURSE
[From within] Madam!

JULIET
                              Be there right away—
You cease your quest and leave me to my grief.
Tomorrow I'll send word.

ROMEO
That I may live—

JULIET
A thousand times good night!

[Exit]

ROMEO
A thousand one times worse to lack your light!   155
Love goes toward love like schoolboys fleeing books,
But turns from love towards school with heavy looks.

[ROMEO withdraws slowly]
[Re-enter JULIET, above]

JULIET
Psst! Romeo, psst!—Give me a hunter's yell
To call this princely falcon back again!
In bondage we are hushed and can't cry out   160
Or in that cave where Echo mourns Narcissus,
I'd make her whispery tongue more hoarse than mine
With repetition of "My Romeo."

ROMEO
It is my soul that's calling out my name.
How silver-sweet sound lovers' tongues at night,   165
Like softest music to attentive ears!

JULIET
Romeo!

ROMEO
My nestling?

JULIET
At what time tomorrow
Should I send word to you?

ROMEO
At nine o'clock.

JULIET
I will not fail. It's twenty years till then.
I have forgotten why I called you back. 170

ROMEO
Let me stand here till you remember why.

JULIET
Then I'll forget, and keep you standing there,
Remembering how I love your company.

ROMEO
Forever I will stay, so you'll forget,
Forget there's any other home but this. 175

JULIET
It's almost dawn. I'd like for you to go,
And yet no farther than a brat's poor bird,
Who lets it hop a little from his hand,
Like a poor prisoner twisting in his chains,
Who with a silk thread yanks it back again, 180
And out of love restricts its liberty.

ROMEO
I wish I were your bird.

JULIET
                    Dear, so do I,
Though I might kill you with my warm embrace.
Good night, good night! Parting is such sweet sorrow
That I could say "Good night" until tomorrow. 185

[Exit]

ROMEO
Sleep dwell within your eyes, peace in your breast!
If I were sleep and peace, how sweet to rest!
From here I'll go to my confessor's cell,
His help I'll seek, and my good luck I'll tell.

[Exit]

Scene Three. Friar Lawrence's Cell

[Enter FRIAR LAWRENCE with a basket]

FRIAR LAWRENCE
The gray-eyed morn smiles on the frowning night,
Slicing the eastern clouds with streaks of light,
And mottled darkness like a drunkard reels
From daylight's path and Titan's fiery wheels.³
Before the sun can raise its burning eye,   5
To cheer the day and drink the night's dew dry,
I must fill up this wicker crate of ours
With toxic weeds and precious-nectared flowers.
The earth, our natural mother, is a tomb;
What is her burying ground serves as her womb;   10
And from her womb come children of all kinds,
All sucking from her natural breast one finds,
Many with many powers excellent,
Not one without one, yet all different.
Each plant and herb and stone, innate in it,   15
There lies some rich medicinal benefit.
For on this earth the vilest things that live
Add to the earth some special good they give;
And every good when stretched past proper use,
Rejects its nature, stumbling on abuse.   20
A virtue turns to vice, when misapplied;
Acts born of vice are sometimes dignified.

[Enter ROMEO]

Within the infant bud of this small flower
Resides a poison and a healing power:
If it is sniffed, one sense is overjoyed;   25
If tasted, then all senses are destroyed.
These two opposing kings contest this place
In man as well as herbs—brute will and grace;
And anywhere the worst comes out on top,
The canker worm will soon wipe out the crop.   30

ROMEO
Good morning, father!

FRIAR LAWRENCE
    Benedicite.
What early tongue's so sweetly greeting me?
Young man, it indicates a troubled head
To say goodbye this early to your bed.
Unease stands watch in every old man's eye,   35
And where it beds down sleep will never lie;
But where an unbruised youth with unstuffed brain
Plops down his limbs, there golden sleep will reign.
And since you're up so early, I attest
Some turbulence in you disturbed your rest;   40
If that's not so, then now I've guessed it right:
Our Romeo has not been in bed tonight.

ROMEO
The last is true. A sweeter peace was mine.

FRIAR LAWRENCE
God pardon sin! Were you with Rosaline?

ROMEO
With Rosaline, my holy father? No.   45
I have forgot that name, and all its woe.

FRIAR LAWRENCE
That's good my son. But then where have you been?

ROMEO
I'll tell you—you won't need to ask again.
I have been feasting with my enemy,
Where one, all of a sudden, wounded me   50
Whom I have wounded too. What we endure,
Your holy medicine will surely cure.
I bear no hatred, blessed man—Oh, no—
For my petition likewise aids my foe.

FRIAR LAWRENCE
Speak plainly, son, without circumlocution—   55
Puzzling confession, puzzling absolution.

ROMEO
The plain truth is my dear heart's love is set
On the fair daughter of rich Capulet.
As mine is set on hers, hers is on mine,
And all is joined, save what you must combine   60
By holy marriage. When, and where, and how
We met and courted, and exchanged our vow,
I'll tell you as we go, but this I pray,
That you'll consent to marry us today.

FRIAR LAWRENCE
Holy Saint Francis! What a change is here!   65
Is Rosaline, whom you just loved so dear,
So quickly cast aside? Young men's love lies
Not truly in their hearts, but in their eyes.
Jesu Maria, think of all the brine
That rinsed your sallow cheeks for Rosaline!   70
How much salt water thrown away in waste,
To marinate a love it did not taste!
The sun has not yet cleared away your sighs,
Your frown still glares into my ancient eyes.
Look there, right on your face I see the streaks   75
Of some old tears still not washed off your cheeks.
If you are you, and your grief's genuine
You and your grief were meant for Rosaline.
Could you have changed? Repeat this maxim then:
Women may fall, when there's no strength in men.   80

ROMEO
For loving Rosaline, a reprimand.

FRIAR LAWRENCE
For doting, not for loving—understand.

ROMEO
And told to bury love.

FRIAR LAWRENCE
                    Not in a tomb,
To toss out one, so others will have room.

ROMEO
Don't scold me, please. The one I love, you see,   85
Gives love for love and also favors me,
Not like the other one.

FRIAR LAWRENCE
                    She knew too well
You cite your love by rote, yet cannot spell.
But come, my wavering one, let's work on this.
There is one reason why I should assist,   90
For this alliance may turn out to be
A means to change discord to harmony.

ROMEO
Then let us hurry. There's no time to waste.

FRIAR LAWRENCE
Wisely, and slow. I've stumbled when I've raced.

                    [Exit]

Scene Four. A Street

          [Enter BENVOLIO and MERCUTIO]

MERCUTIO
Where the devil could this Romeo be?
Did he go home last night?

BENVOLIO
Not to his father's. I spoke with his servant.

MERCUTIO
Why, it's that pale, hard-hearted wench, that Rosaline.
She torments him so much he'll soon go mad.   5

BENVOLIO
Tybalt, the kinsman to old Capulet,
Has sent a letter to his father's house.

MERCUTIO
A challenge, I am sure.

BENVOLIO
Romeo will answer it.

MERCUTIO
Any man that can write can answer a letter.   10

BENVOLIO
No, he will answer the letter's master, daring him now
that he's dared.

MERCUTIO
Alas, poor Romeo, he is already dead! Stabbed by a pale
wench's black eye, shot through the ear with a love song,
his heart's bull's-eye cleft by the blind bow-boy's barbed   15
shaft. Is he the man to take on Tybalt?

BENVOLIO
Tybalt? My kitten's named King Tybalt.

MERCUTIO
He's more than a prince of kittens, I tell you—an ever-
fearless ensign of fencing etiquette. He fights as you
might finger a flute—keeps time, distance, and rhythm; a   20
sixteenth note rest, then a grace note—one, two, the third
goes in your breast—the very butcher of a silk button, a
"duelettante", yes a "duelettante"; a gentleman of the very
best school, provoked by insult and honor. [acts out dueling
moves] Ah, the immortal *passado*! The *punto reverso*! The   25
hay—

BENVOLIO
The what?

MERCUTIO
A pox on these goofy, lisping, affected fops, these fine-
tuners of fancy phrases! What's wrong with saying "a very
good sword! A very tall man! A very good whore!" Isn't it   30
something to lament, old man, that we are afflicted with
these alien flies, these fashion-mongers, these "oh, *pardon-
moi's*," with their *bon* this and their *bon* that—sporting so
many "*bons*" they can't fit comfortably in their old pants?
O my bones, my bones.   35

[Enter ROMEO, still wearing his costume]

BENVOLIO
Here comes Romeo, here comes Romeo!

MERCUTIO
Without his roe, I bet, like a dried up herring. O flesh,
flesh, how fishified you look! Now he is floating in one of
Petrarch's sonnets, whose love, compared to his lady, was
just a kitchen wench—even if he was better at rhyming her   40
with things; Venus, a vixen; Cleopatra, a party girl; Dido,
debauched; Helen, a harlot, a blue eye or two, but nothing
else worth mentioning. Signior Romeo, bon jour! A French
hello for that French slip you're wearing. You sure gave us
the slip last night.   45

ROMEO
Good morning to you both. What slip did I give you?

MERCUTIO
The slip, sir, the slip. Don't you get it?

ROMEO
Pardon me, Mercutio. I've been deeply engaged, and in such
a case as mine a man may relax the rules of etiquette.

MERCUTIO
I'd think a deep engagement such as yours might tighten   50
the hamstrings a bit.

ROMEO
I mean I was tied up.

MERCUTIO
Now you're getting it.

ROMEO
A polite way of putting it.

MERCUTIO
Yes, I am the very essence of politeness.   55

ROMEO
Essence as in aroma.

MERCUTIO
Right.

ROMEO
Well then, my shoes are very polite.

MERCUTIO
Well done. Let's keep up this banter until you've worn out
your shoes, which, judging by their flimsy soles, may wear   60
out before this joke does.

ROMEO
A flimsy joke, its sole lined only with silliness.

MERCUTIO
Be my second in this duel, Benvolio. My wit is fading.

ROMEO
More spur, more whip, or I'll claim victory.

MERCUTIO
No, if I follow your lead, this wild goose chase will do me in,   65
for you have more wild geese to chase in an ounce of your
mind, I am sure, than I have in all of mine. Has this goose
line caught me up to you?

ROMEO
A goose gets in its best digs when it's behind.

MERCUTIO
I will peck you on the cheek for that dig.   70

ROMEO
Please, no pecks from you, good goose.

MERCUTIO
Your wit's a very bitter apple; too sour for my taste.

ROMEO
But tasty when served with such a sweet goose.

MERCUTIO
Your wit's a scrap of cloth you stretch from inches into
yards.   75

ROMEO
Just enough to make a pillow case to stuff your feathers in
when I'm finished with you.

MERCUTIO
Now isn't this better than whining for love? You're sociable
again. Now you are Romeo; now you are what you are,
shaped by art as well as nature, for this drooling love is   80
like a big, slobbering idiot that runs back and forth looking
for a hole to shake his rattle in.

BENVOLIO
Stop there, stop there.

MERCUTIO
Cut off my tale while it's down a hole?

BENVOLIO
Well, it's long enough as it is.   85

MERCUTIO
You're all mixed up. The whole of my tale, once it's reached, is that it gets no longer and is soon finished. I had no intention of dwelling there long.

ROMEO
Here's some ample apparel.

[Enter NURSE and PETER]

Sail, ho! Sail, ho!   90

MERCUTIO
No, two. One shirt, one skirt.

NURSE
Peter!

PETER (Servant of Juliet's nurse)
Coming.

NURSE
My fan, Peter.

MERCUTIO
Quick, Peter, to hide her face, for her fan's the fairer of   95
the two.

NURSE
Good morning to you, gentlemen.

MERCUTIO
Good afternoon, fair gentlewoman.

NURSE
Is it afternoon?

MERCUTIO
Way past for you, I tell you, for the bawdy hand of the dial   100
is giving the finger to the twelve.

NURSE
Disgusting! What sort of man are you?

ROMEO
One, gentlewoman, made in God's image only to abuse
himself.

NURSE
That's the truth. "To abuse himself," indeed. Gentlemen, can   105
any of you tell me where I may find the young Romeo?

ROMEO
I can tell you, but young Romeo will be older when you find
him than he was when you sought him. I am the youngest
with that name, for lack of a worse one.

NURSE
That's better.   110

MERCUTIO
Is a worse one better? Better think about it.

NURSE
If you are he, sir, I desire to confiscate with you.

BENVOLIO
She will "invitate" him to her party.

MERCUTIO
A tart, a tart, a tart! Tally ho!

ROMEO
What have you found?   115

MERCUTIO
[sizing up NURSE] Not really a plum one, sir, unless by tart
we mean a pastry, one a bit too old and moldy to sell.
[Sings]
    An old stale tart,
    Yes, an old stale tart,
    In lean times may suffice   120
    But a tart that's stale
    And up for sale
    Cannot be worth the price.
Romeo, let's go to your father's house? We'll have dinner
there.   125

ROMEO
Go ahead. I'll follow.

MERCUTIO
Farewell, ancient lady. [singing] "Farewell, lady, lady,
lady."

                [Exit MERCUTIO and BENVOLIO]

NURSE
Tell me, sir, who is that smart-mouthed character who's so
proud of his ribaldry?   130

ROMEO
A gentleman, nurse, who loves to hear himself talk and
will say more in a minute than he could rise to defend in
a month.

NURSE
If he says anything against me, I'll deflate him, even if he's
harder than he looks, and there were twenty such rascals. 135
And if I cannot, I'll find some that can. Scurvy knave! I am
not one of his floozies, one of his cutthroat tagalongs. [To
PETER] And you just stand there and allow every knave
to use me as he pleases!

PETER
I saw no man use you as he pleased. If I had, my weapon 140
would quickly have been out, I guarantee you. I draw as
soon as any other man, if I see an opportunity for a good
scuffle, and if the law is on my side.

NURSE
Now, before God, I am so aroused that every part of me is
throbbing. Scurvy knave! [to ROMEO] Please, sir, a word 145
with you. As I tried to tell you, my young lady has requested
me to look you up. What she told me to say I will keep to
myself, but first let me tell you, if you lead her into a fool's
paradise, as they say, it'd be a very gross kind of behavior,
as they say. For the gentlewoman is young; and, therefore, 150
if you double deal with her, it is truly a wicked thing to do
to any gentlewoman, and very shameful treatment.

ROMEO
Nurse, convey my respects to your lady and mistress. I
profess to you...

NURSE
[interrupts] A good man, and you can bet I will tell her 155
that. Lord, Lord, she will be a joyful woman.

ROMEO
What will you tell her, nurse? You cut me off.

NURSE
I will tell her, sir, that you have professed, which, as I see
it, is a gentlemanly offer.

ROMEO
Have her arrange this afternoon to make confession,   160
And there she will in Friar Lawrence' cell
Be blessed and married. This is for your help. [offers
    coins]

NURSE
No, truly, sir. Not a penny.

ROMEO
Come on. I must insist.

NURSE
This afternoon, sir? Well, she shall be there.   165

ROMEO
And stay, good nurse, behind the abbey-wall.
My servant in an hour will contact you,
And bring a ladder made from knotted rope
To reach the highest mast of all my joy,
My passage in the cover of the night.   170
Farewell. Be true, and I'll reward your pains.
Farewell. And give your mistress my regards.

NURSE
Now God in heaven bless you! Listen, sir.

ROMEO
What is it, my dear nurse?

NURSE
Is your man trustworthy? I've heard it said,   175
Two can keep secrets, long as both are dead.

ROMEO
I promise you, my man's as true as steel.

NURSE
Well, sir, my mistress is the sweetest lady.—Lord, Lord,
when she was a little prattling thing—O, there was a
nobleman in town, named Paris, who had staked her out, 180
but she, good soul, would have been quicker to look at a
toad, yes a toad, than look at him. I tease her sometimes,
and tell her that Paris is the handsomest man, but I have
you know, when I say that, she looks as pale as any sheet
in the entire world. Don't rosemary and Romeo begin with 185
the same letter?[4]

ROMEO
Yes, nurse; what of it? Both with R.

NURSE
You tease! "AAR" is what dogs say. No, I know they begin
with some other letter, and she recites such a pretty
abhorism about it, about you and rosemary, that it would 190
do you good to hear it.

ROMEO
Give your mistress my regards.

NURSE
Yes, a thousand times.

[Exit ROMEO]

Peter!

PETER
Coming.   195

NURSE
Peter, take my fan, and get moving.

[Exit NURSE and PETER]

Scene Five. Capulet's Garden

[enter JULIET]

JULIET
The clock struck nine when I sent out the nurse.
In half an hour she promised to return.
Perhaps she could not meet him. That's not so.
She moves so slow! Love's envoys should be thoughts,

Which glide ten times as fast as sunbeams do,   5
Driving back shadows over glowering hills.
That's why love's chariot's drawn by quick-winged doves,
And that's why Cupid, swift as wind, has wings.
The sun is now upon the highest point
Of this day's journey, and from nine till twelve   10
Is three long hours, yet she has not returned.
If she had feelings and warm youthful blood,
She'd be as swift in motion as a ball;
My words would volley her to my sweet love,
And his to me.   15
But old folks, many act as if they're dead.
Unwieldy, slow, and heavy, dull as lead.

[Enter NURSE and PETER].

O God, she's back!—O dearest nurse, what news?
Did you meet with him? Send your man away.

NURSE
Peter, stay at the gate.   20

[Exit PETER]

JULIET
Now, good sweet nurse—O Lord, why look so sad?
Though news is sad, we tell it pleasantly.
If good, you shame the music of sweet news
By playing it with such a sour face.

NURSE
I wore myself out. Let me catch my breath.   25
Lord, how my bones ache! What an expedition!

JULIET
I wish you'd had my bones, and I your news.
Now nurse, please speak to me. Good nurse, please
    speak.

NURSE
Jesus? Why rush? Sit down and stay awhile.
Do you not see that I am out of breath?   30

JULIET
How are you out of breath, when you have breath
Enough to tell me that you're out of breath?
Excuses that you make for this delay
Are longer than the tale that you won't tell.
Is your news good or bad? Just answer that.   35
Say either one, the details then can wait.
At least let me know—is it good or bad?

NURSE
Well, you have made a foolish choice. You don't know how
to choose a man. Romeo? No, not him. Though his face is
better than any man's, and his legs excel all men's, and   40
as for his hands and feet and body, though not polite to
mention, they are beyond compare. Not the best example
of courtesy, but I'm sure he's as gentle as a lamb. So that's
that, wench, best go and serve God. Well, have you dined
at home?   45

JULIET
No, no, no. All of this I knew before.
What word about our marriage? What of that?

NURSE
Lord, how my head aches! What a head I have!
It beats as if it broke in twenty pieces.   50
And then there is my back. O, my back, my back!
Shame on your heart for sending me out there
To catch my death by trudging up and down.

JULIET
Truly, I'm sorry that you are not well.
Sweet, sweet, nurse. Tell me what my love has said?   55

NURSE
Your love said, like an honest gentleman, and a courteous,

and a kind, and a handsome, and, I am sure, a virtuous
...Where is your mother?

JULIET
Where is my mother? Why, she is inside.
Where should she be? How oddly you reply: 60
[mocking] "Your love said, like an honest gentleman,
'Where is your mother?' "

NURSE
                    By the blessed virgin!
A bit on edge, Miss High and Mighty one?
Is this the way to treat my aching bones?
From now on, send your messages yourself.   65

JULIET
Why all this fuss! Come, what did Romeo say?

NURSE
Can you find time to go make your confession?

JULIET
I can.

NURSE
Then quickly go to Friar Lawrence's cell.
A husband waits there to make you his wife.   70
Here comes the wayward blood back to your cheeks;
They surge to scarlet at a hint of news.
Go quick to church. I'll go another way,
To fetch a ladder here, so that your love
Can reach the bird's nest soon as it is dark.   75
I am a drudge who toils for your delight.
But you will bear the weight of it tonight.
Go. I'll have dinner. Hurry to the cell.

JULIET
And to good fortune!—Treasured nurse, farewell.

[Exit]

Scene Six. Friar Lawrence's Cell

[Enter FRIAR LAWRENCE and ROMEO]

FRIAR LAWRENCE
If heaven smiles upon this holy act
The aftermath won't punish us with grief.

ROMEO
Amen, amen. But sorrow, if it comes
Cannot outweigh this fair exchange of joy
Which one short minute in her sight gives me.   5
If you'll just join our hands with holy words,
Then love-devouring death can have its way—
It is enough for me to call her mine.

FRIAR LAWRENCE
These violent delights have violent ends,
And die in triumph like sparks hitting powder,   10
Which, as they kiss, ignite. The sweetest honey
Is sickeningly delicious by itself,
And tasting it destroys the appetite.
Therefore, love moderately. Long love does that.
For those too swift can fall behind the slow.   15

[Enter JULIET]

Here comes the lady. Footsteps light as these
Will never wear away immortal stone.
A lover may traverse the dainty webs
That idly float in playful summer air
And yet not fall, so light is earthly love.   20

JULIET
Good afternoon to you my holy father.

FRIAR LAWRENCE
Romeo will kiss you, daughter, for us both.

JULIET
And I'll kiss him, or I'll be overpaid.

ROMEO
Ah, Juliet, if you measure out your joy
In heaps like mine, and if you have more skill   25
At praising it, then sweeten with your breath
The neighboring air, and let your tongue's rich song
Expose the held-in happiness that both
Of us receive from such a dear encounter.

JULIET
Imagined love, when richer than mere words,   30
Delights in substance, not in ornament.
Like beggars, words can easily count their worth,
But my true love has grown to such extremes,
I can't sum up the sum of half my wealth.

FRIAR LAWRENCE
Come, come with me, we'll make short work of this.   35
With your consent, you'd best not be alone
Till holy marriage joins two into one.

[Exit]

Romeo and Juliet

Act Three

Act Three

Scene One. A Public Place

[Enter MERCUTIO, BENVOLIO, PAGE,
and SERVANTS]

BENVOLIO
Mercutio, I beg you, let's go in.
The day is hot, the Capulets are out,
And if we meet, we can't avoid a brawl,
For these hot days now stir the blood to passion.

MERCUTIO
You are like one of these fellows who, when he enters the   5
confines of a tavern, slaps his sword upon the table, and
says to it "God gave me no need for you!" But when the
second cup goes to work, he waves it at the waiter, when
indeed there is no need.

BENVOLIO
Am I such a fellow?   10

MERCUTIO
Come, come, you have as hot a temper as any Joe in Italy—
one minute moved to be mad, the next mad to be moved.

BENVOLIO
Am I both?

MERCUTIO
You can't be both. If there were two such types, we would
soon have none, for one would kill the other. You—Why,   15

you will pick a fight with any man with one hair more or one hair less in his beard than you have. You will fight a man for cracking hazel nuts, only because that's the color of your eyes. What eye but that eye could spot so many opportunities for a fight? Your head is as full of quarrels as   20
an egg is full of yoke, and yet your head has been beaten as rotten as an egg from fighting. You have fought a man for coughing in the street because he woke up your dog which was sleeping in the sun. Didn't you clash with a tailor for wearing a new jacket before Easter? With a shoemaker   25
for tying his new shoes with old laces? And yet you warn me about fighting!

BENVOLIO
If I were as quick to fight as you are, the lease on my life would not last an hour and a quarter.

MERCUTIO
The lease! The least thing upsets you!   30

BENVOLIO
Bless my soul, here come the Capulets.

MERCUTIO
Bless my boot heel, I could care less.

[Enter TYBALT, PETRUCHIO and others]

TYBALT
Follow me closely, I will speak to them. Gentlemen, good day. A word with one of you.

MERCUTIO
And just one word with one of us? Invite another along.   35
Make it a word and a blow.

TYBALT
You will find me ready enough for that, sir, if you give me any occasion to.

MERCUTIO
Could the occasion arise without me giving you one?

TYBALT
Mercutio, you belong to Romeo's choir. 40

MERCUTIO
Choir! So you see us as choir boys? If you think we're the
choir, expect to hear nothing but sour notes. Here's the bow
I fiddle with. [gestures toward his sword] This will make
you dance. Bloody Christ, choir! Choir!

BENVOLIO
We're talking in a very public place. 45
Either withdraw into some private place,
And calmly work out all your grievances,
Or else depart. Here all eyes gaze on us.

MERCUTIO
Men's eyes were made to look, so let them gaze.
I will not budge to please a man, not I. 50

[Enter ROMEO]

TYBALT
Sir, peace be with you.—This one suits me more.

MERCUTIO
Well, I'll be hanged if he's the one who dressed you.
Go to the dueling field, he'll press your suit.
You'll find him waiting on your Worship there.

TYBALT
Romeo, the love I feel for you can yield 55
No better term than this: you are a villain.

ROMEO
Tybalt, the reason why I have to love you
Relieves somewhat the need for proper rage

At such a greeting. Villain I am not.
And so, farewell. You don't know me, that's clear.   60

TYBALT
Boy, this does not relieve the injuries
That you have given me. So turn and draw.

ROMEO
I must insist I've never injured you
But love you more than you can realize
Until you learn the reason for my love.   65
And so good Capulet—a name I value
As dearly as my own—be satisfied.

MERCUTIO
A calm, dishonorable, vile submission!
And Mr. Catscratch walks off with the win. [Draws]
Tybalt, you rat-catcher, just name the place!   70

TYBALT
What do you want from me?

MERCUTIO
Good king of kittens, nothing but one of your nine lives,
which I intend to snatch from you, and, depending on your
treatment of me, thrash the other eight. Will you pluck your
sword from its pouch by the tail? Better hurry, or mine will   75
make it a short one.

TYBALT
I'm ready for you. [Drawing]

ROMEO
Gentle Mercutio, put your sword away.

MERCUTIO
Come, sir, show me your *passado.*

[They fight]

ROMEO
Draw, Benvolio; knock down their weapons.   80
Gentlemen, this is shameful! Cease this outrage!
Tybalt! Mercutio! The prince expressly has
Forbid such bandying in Verona's streets.

[ROMEO steps between them and holds MERCUTIO]

Stop, Tybalt! Good Mercutio!

[TYBALT stabs MERCUTIO and
flees with his followers]]

PETRUCHIO (friend of Tybalt)
Let's go, Tybalt.   85

MERCUTIO
I am hurt.
A plague on both your houses! I am spent.
Is he gone? Did I miss him?

BENVOLIO
                      What, are you hurt?

MERCUTIO
Yes, yes, a scratch, a scratch, but it's enough.
Where is my page? Go, fellow, fetch a surgeon.   90

[Exit PAGE]

ROMEO
Courage, man. The wound cannot be much.

MERCUTIO
No, it's not as deep as a well, nor as wide as a church door,
but it's enough. It will do. Ask for me tomorrow, and you'll
find a grave man. I am ruined, I am sure, for this world.
A plague on both your houses! Bloody Christ, a dog, a rat,   95
a mouse, a cat can scratch a man to death! A braggart, a
rogue, a villain, who fights out of a fencing manual! Why

the devil did you step between us? I was hurt while you
held me.

ROMEO
I thought it for the best.   100

MERCUTIO
Help me into some house, Benvolio,
Or I will faint. A plague on both your houses!
They've made me into worm meat.
I got it...soundly too. Your houses!

[Exit MERCUTIO and BENVOLIO]

ROMEO
This gentleman, the prince's closest kin,   105
My truest friend, received a mortal wound
On my behalf. My reputation stained
By Tybalt's slander—Tybalt, for one hour,
Has been my kinsman. O sweet Juliet,
Your beauty has made me effeminate   110
And softened up my valor's tempered steel.

[Re-enter BENVOLIO]

BENVOLIO
O Romeo, Romeo, brave Mercutio's dead!
That gallant spirit now ascends the clouds,
Which much too soon came here to scorn the earth.

ROMEO
Today's black fate—more days like this portend.   115
What this begins the rest of us must end.

[Re-enter TYBALT]

BENVOLIO
That furious Tybalt's coming back again.

ROMEO
Again in triumph, and Mercutio slain!
Let heaven judge the case for leniency,
And fire-eyed fury, you are now my guide!   120
Now, Tybalt, take the title "villain" back
That you just gave me, for Mercutio's soul
Is now a little ways above our heads,
Waiting for you to keep him company.
Either you or I, or both, must go with him.   125

TYBALT
You, wretched boy, who joined his choir here,
Will join him there.

ROMEO
                        This will determine that.

[ROMEO draws his sword]
[They fight; TYBALT falls and dies]

BENVOLIO
Romeo, away, be gone!
The public's up in arms. And Tybalt's dead.
Don't stand there shocked. The prince will capture you   130
And sentence you to death. Be gone, away!

ROMEO
O, I am fortune's fool!

BENVOLIO
                        You cannot stay!

[Exit ROMEO]
[Enter CITIZENS]

1ST CITIZEN
The one that killed Mercutio, where'd he go?
Tybalt, that murderer, which way'd he run?

BENVOLIO
He's lying there. [kneels beside TYBALT]

1ˢᵗ CITIZEN
                    Get up, sir, come with me.   135
By order of the prince you must obey.

            [Enter PRINCE ESCALUS, with attendants;
        MONTAGUE, CAPULET, their WIVES, and others]

PRINCE ESCALUS
Where are the instigators of this fray?

BENVOLIO
O noble prince. I can reveal to all
The fatal course of this unlucky brawl.
There lies the man, slain by young Romeo,   140
That slew your kinsman, brave Mercutio.

LADY CAPULET
Tybalt, my kin! My brother's child is killed!
O prince, O husband! O, the blood is spilled
Of my dear kinsman! Prince, your judgment's true,
For blood of ours shed blood of Montague.   145
O nephew, nephew!

PRINCE ESCALUS
Benvolio, who began this bloody fray?

BENVOLIO
Tybalt, whom Romeo then was forced to slay.
Romeo spoke kindly, pointing out to him
How petty this fight was, and warned him of   150
Your great displeasure. All of this—expressed
With gentle breath, calm looks, knees humbly bent—
Could not make peace with the unruly wrath
Of Tybalt, who's so deaf to peace, he strikes
With piercing steel at brave Mercutio's breast,   155
Who, now hot too, meets deadly point with point,

And, with a warrior's scorn, with one hand sweeps
Cold death aside, and with the other sends
It back to Tybalt, whose dexterity
Replies in kind. And Romeo then cries out,   160
"Wait, friends! Friends, part!" and swifter than his
     tongue,
His agile arm knocks down their lethal points,
And leaps between them; underneath his arm
A spiteful thrust from Tybalt takes the life
Of brave Mercutio, and then Tybalt flees,   165
But right away comes back at Romeo,
Who only then was thinking of revenge,
And go at it like lightning; by the time
I drew to part them Tybalt had been slain,
And as he fell, then Romeo turned and fled.   170
This is the truth, or strike Benvolio dead.

LADY CAPULET
He is a nephew of old Montague,
Close kinship means he cannot say what's true.
Some twenty of them fought in this black strife,
And all those twenty only took one life.   175
I beg for justice, which you, prince, must give.
Romeo slew Tybalt, Romeo must not live.

PRINCE ESCALUS
Romeo slew him; he slew Mercutio.
The debt for his dear blood someone must owe.

MONTAGUE
Not Romeo, prince; he was Mercutio's friend.   180
His error just closes what the law would end,
The life of Tybalt.

PRINCE ESCALUS
                    And for this disgrace
Immediately he's exiled from this place.
I'm now involved in where you hate is leading:
Due to these brawls my own blood lies there bleeding,   185

But I will hit you with so strong a fine
That you will all repent this loss of mine.
I will be deaf to pleading and excuses,
No tears or prayers can put right such abuses,
So save them and have Romeo leave here fast,   190
Or, when he's found, that hour will be his last.
Remove this body, and obey my will.
By pardoning murder, mercy too can kill.

[Exit]

Scene Two. A Room in Capulet's House

[Enter JULIET]

JULIET
Gallop apace, you fiery-footed steeds,
To where the Sun God sleeps. The charioteer,
His son, would whip you west, you runaways,
And bring in cloudy night immediately.
Close your concealing drapes, love-harboring night!   5
So renegade eyes will blink,[1] and Romeo
Can leap into these arms, unheard, unseen.
Lovers can carry out their amorous rites
By their own beauty's glow, or, if love's blind,
It best agrees with night. Come, somber night,   10
You sober-suited matron, all in black,
And teach me how to lose a winning match,
Played by a pair of virgins still unstained.
Riderless blood, stampeding in my cheeks,
Keep blinders on, till timid love, grown bold,   15
Sees acts of love as harmless chastity.
Come, night. Come, Romeo. Come, my day in night,
For you will lie upon the wings of night
Whiter than new snow upon a raven's back.
Come, gentle night, come loving, black-browed night,   20
Give me my Romeo, and when I die,

Take him and cut him into little stars,
And he will make the heaven's face so fine
That all the world will be in love with night
And pay no worship to the glaring sun.   25
O, I have bought a mansion full of love,
But don't possess it yet, and though I'm sold,
Not yet enjoyed. So tedious is this day,
As is the night before some festival
To an impatient child who has new clothes,   30
And may not wear them.

[Enter NURSE, with ropes]

                              O, here comes my nurse,
And she brings news; each tongue that merely says
His name now sounds divinely eloquent.
Now, nurse, what news? What's that you have? The ropes
That Romeo said to bring?

NURSE

                              Ay, ay, the ropes.   35

              [Drops down the rope ladder]

JULIET
Ah yes! What news? Why did you wring your hands?

NURSE
Ah, woe this day! He's dead, he's dead, he's dead!
We're done for, lady, we are done for now.
Terrible day. He's gone, he's killed, he's dead!

JULIET
Can heaven be so spiteful?

NURSE
                              Romeo can,   40
Though heaven cannot. O Romeo, Romeo!
Who ever would have thought it? Romeo!

JULIET
What kind of fiend would torment me like this?
This torture should come screeching out of hell.
Has Romeo slain himself? If you say "Ay",   45
Then that lone vowel "I" will poison more
Than the death-darting eyes of Gorgon's head.
I am not I if there's that kind of I,
Or his are shut and make you answer "Ay."
If he is slain, say "Ay" or if not, "No."   50
Brief sounds determine my well-being or woe.

NURSE
I saw the wound, I saw it with my eyes—
May God protect me—in his manly breast.
A piteous corpse, a bloody piteous corpse,
Pale, pale as ashes, all bedaubed in blood,   55
In clotted blood. I fainted at the sight.

JULIET
O, break, my heart, go bankrupt, break for good!
To prison, eyes; see liberty no more!
Vile stuff, return to dust, all motion cease;
One stretcher take us both to rest in peace!   60

NURSE
O Tybalt, Tybalt, the best friend I had!
O kindly Tybalt! Honorable man!
I never thought I'd live to see you dead!

JULIET
What storm is this that blows so many ways?
Is Romeo slaughtered, and is Tybalt dead?   65
Both my dear cousin, and my dearer lord?
Then, dreadful trumpet, sound the judgment day,
For who is living, if those two are gone?

NURSE
Tybalt is gone, and Romeo...banishment.
Romeo's who killed him, so it's banishment.   70

JULIET
O God, did Romeo's hand shed Tybalt's blood?

NURSE
It did, it did; o woe the day, it did.

JULIET
A serpent's heart, with flowers for a face!
Has any dragon had so fine a cave?
Beautiful tyrant! Fiend angelical!   75
Dove-feathered raven! Wolfish-ravenous lamb!
Despicable within, divine without!
The clear reverse of what you clearly seem,
A saint who's damned, an honorable villain.
O nature, what did hell have you create   80
When you enshrined the spirit of a fiend
In mortal paradise of such sweet flesh?
Are any books containing such vile matter
So nicely bound? O, that deceit should dwell
In such a gorgeous palace!

NURSE
                There's no trust,   85
No faith, no honesty in men. All liars,
All perjurers, all wicked, all dissemblers.
Where's Peter? Bring some aqueous reviver.
These griefs, these woes, these sorrows make me old.
Shame come to Romeo!

JULIET
                Blisters on your tongue   90
For such a wish! His birthright is not shame.
Upon his head shame is ashamed to sit,
For it's a throne where honour should be crowned
Sole monarch of this earthly universe.
O, what a beast I was to chide him so!   95

NURSE
Can you speak well of one who killed your cousin?

JULIET
Can I speak ill of one who is my husband?
Ah, my poor lord, what tongue restores your name,
When I, a three-hour wife, have mangled it?
But why, you devil, did you kill my cousin?   100
That devilish cousin would have killed my husband.
Back, foolish tears, back to your native spring;
Your drops are tributaries feeding grief,
Which, by mistake, you offer up in joy.
My husband lives, whom Tybalt would have slain.   105
And Tybalt's dead, who would have slain my husband.
All this brings comfort. Why then do I weep?
There was one word, much worse than Tybalt's death,
That murdered me. It's best that I forget.
But, O, it presses on my memory   110
Like guilty, damning deeds in sinners' minds:
"Tybalt is dead, and Romeo...banishment."
It's "banishment," that one word "banishment"
Could slay ten thousand Tybalts. Tybalt's death
Was woe enough, if it had ended there,   115
Or, if sour woes delight in company,
And need to form in ranks with other griefs,
Why not throw in, when she said Tybalt's dead,
Your father, or your mother, even both,
Which prompts an ordinary show of grief?   120
But with a rear-guard following Tybalt's death,
His "banishment"—that word—why not just say
That father, mother, Tybalt, Romeo, Juliet,
All slain, all dead. "Romeo...banishment"—
There is no end, no limit, measure, bounds,   125
No word can plumb the depths of that word's sound.
Where are my father and my mother, nurse?

NURSE
Weeping and wailing over Tybalt's body.
Will you go to them? I will take you there.

JULIET
Their tears can wash his wounds. Mine will be spent,   130

When theirs are dry, on Romeo's banishment.
Remove these ropes. Poor ropes, you've been beguiled,
Both you and I, for Romeo's exiled.
With you he made a highway to my bed,
But I will die, a widowed maid instead.   135
Come, ropes—Come, nurse. Come to my wedding-bed,
And death, not Romeo, take my maidenhead!

NURSE
Rush to your chamber. I'll find Romeo
To comfort you: I know right where he is.
Now listen, Romeo will be here tonight: 140
I'll go to him. He's at the Friar's cell.

JULIET
O, find him! Give this ring to my true knight.
Tell him to come and make his last farewell.

[Exit]

Scene Three. Friar Lawrence's Cell

[Enter FRIAR LAWRENCE]

FRIAR LAWRENCE
Romeo, come out; come out, you frightened man.
Disaster has been smitten with your charms,
And you are wedded to calamity.

[Enter ROMEO]

ROMEO
Is there news, father? What's the prince's judgment?
What eager sorrow yearns to shake my hand   5
That I don't know of?

FRIAR LAWRENCE
                    Too familiar now

Is my dear son with such sour company.
I bring you word on what that judgment is.

ROMEO
His judgment surely means my judgment day.

FRIAR LAWRENCE
A gentler judgment wafted from his lips: 10
Not bodily death, but bodily banishment.

ROMEO
Ha, banishment? Be merciful, say death,
For exile has more terror in its face,
Much more than death. Do not say banishment.

FRIAR LAWRENCE
You're banished from Verona from now on.   15
Compose yourself, the world is broad and wide.

ROMEO
There is no world without Verona's walls,
Just purgatory, torture, hell itself.
Banished from here is banished from the world,
And worldwide exile's death. So banishment   20
Is death misnamed. Calling death banishment,
You chop my head off with a golden axe,
While smiling at the stroke that murders me.

FRIAR LAWRENCE
O deadly sin! O rude ungratefulness!
Your crime should call for death, but the kind prince,   25
Taking your side, has pushed aside the law,
And changed that black word death to banishment.
This is rare mercy, yet you can't see that.

ROMEO
It's torture, and not mercy. Heaven's here,
Where Juliet lives, and every cat, and dog,   30
And little mouse, every unworthy thing,
Lives here in heaven, and may look on her,

But Romeo may not. More dignity,
More honored rank, more courtly conduct lives
In carrion flies than Romeo. They may land   35
On the white wonder of dear Juliet's hand,
And steal immortal blessings from her lips,
Which blush in pure and virgin modesty,
For thinking that these kisses are a sin.
But Romeo may not. He's banished now.   40
This, flies may do, while I must fly from this.
And yet you say that exile is not death!
If you had poisons mixed, or knives honed sharp,
Or sudden means of death, none are as mean
As banishment to kill me. Banishment?   45
O friar, the damned will use that word in hell,
Accompanied by howls. How could the heart
Of a divine and spiritual confessor,
A sin-absolver and acknowledged friend,
So mangle me with that word "banishment"?   50

FRIAR LAWRENCE
You foolish, angry man, just listen now.

ROMEO
O, you will speak again of banishment.

FRIAR LAWRENCE
I'll give you armor to fend off that word,
Adversity's sweet milk, philosophy,
To comfort you, though you face banishment.   55

ROMEO
Yet I'm still banished. Hang it on a wall.
Unless philosophy can make a Juliet,
Transplant a town, reverse a prince's verdict,
It does not help, of no avail, no more.

FRIAR LAWRENCE
O, I can see that madmen have no ears.   60

ROMEO
And why should they when wise men have no eyes?

FRIAR LAWRENCE
Let me discuss your situation now.

ROMEO
You cannot speak of what you do not feel.
Were you my age, and Juliet your love,
And married for one hour, when Tybalt's killed,   65
Obsessed like me, like me a banished man,
Then you might speak, and might tear out your hair,
And fall upon the ground, as I do now, [lies down]
So you could measure out your undug grave.

[Knocking offstage]

FRIAR LAWRENCE
Stand up. A knock. Good Romeo, hide yourself.   70

ROMEO
Not I, unless the heartsick groans I breathe,
Conceal me, mist-like, from the search of eyes.

[Knocking]

FRIAR LAWRENCE
Hear how they knock! —Who's there? —Romeo, get up.
You'll be arrested.—Coming!—Now stand up.

[More knocking]

Run to my study—Be right there!—God's will,   75
What foolishness is this.—I'm coming. Coming!

[More knocking]

Who's banging on the door? What brings you here?

NURSE
[Outside] Let me come in, and you shall know my errand.
I come from Lady Juliet.

FRIAR LAWRENCE
          Welcome then.

        [Enter NURSE]

NURSE
O holy friar, O, tell me, holy friar,   80
Where is my lady's lord, where's Romeo?

FRIAR LAWRENCE
There on the ground, and drunk on his own tears.

NURSE
She's in the same position he is in,
And he in hers! In wretched harmony!
Piteous predicament! She lies like that,   85
Blubbering and weeping, weeping and blubbering.—
Rise up, rise up. Rise, if you are a man.
For Juliet's sake, for her sake, rise and stand.
Why fall inside so deep a hole and moan?

        [ROMEO stands up]

ROMEO
Nurse!

NURSE
        Ah sir, ah sir, death's the end for all.   90

ROMEO
Do you mean Juliet? How is it with her?
Does she think I'm a hardened murderer,
Now that I've stained the childhood of our joy
With blood not very far removed from hers?
Where is she? How is she? What does she think   95
Of love that's cancelled while it still concealed?

NURSE
O, she says nothing, sir, just weeps and weeps,

And falls upon her bed, and then leaps up,
Calls Tybalt's name, then cries out Romeo,
Then falls again.

ROMEO
                    It is as if that name,   100
Shot with a dead-eye marksman's point-blank aim,
Has murdered her, just as its curséd hand
Murdered her kinsman.—O, tell me, friar, tell me,
In what vile part of this anatomy
Does my name dwell? Tell me, so I can loot   105
This hateful mansion. [Drawing his sword]

FRIAR LAWRENCE
                    Halt your desperate hand.
Are you a man? Your build suggests you are.
Your tears are girlish; your wild acts display
Unreasoning fury suited to a beast.
Unseemly woman in what seems a man,   110
An aberrant hybrid, seeming girl and beast!
I am astonished. By my holy order,
I thought you had a stronger disposition.
So you've slain Tybalt? Will you slay yourself
And slay this lady, too, who lives in you,   115
By doing to yourself forbidden harm?
Why rail against your birth and heaven and earth
Since birth and heaven and earth, all three will join
In you the moment they are tossed away.
Shame, shame, you shame your body, love, and mind,   120
But like a miser who is rich in these,
You won't employ them in a proper way
That could enhance your body, love, and mind.
Your noble frame is nothing more than wax,
If you evade the valor of real men;   125
This deep, sworn love, no more than hollow lies,
Killing the love which you have vowed to cherish;
Your mind, which should adorn your form and love,
Deformed in how it guides the two of them,
Like powder in a clumsy soldier's flask,   130

Is detonated by your own neglect
With you dismembered by your weaponry.
So, get up, man! Your Juliet is alive,
On whose behalf you wished to kill yourself—
That makes you lucky. Tybalt went at you,   135
But you slew Tybalt—another piece of luck.
The law, which calls for death, became your friend,
And went for exile—that was lucky too.
A pack of blessings lands upon your back,
Happiness courts you in her best attire,   140
But, like a misbehaved and sullen wench,
You frown upon your good luck and your love.
Take heed, take heed, such types die miserably.
Go, go and see your love, as has been planned.
Climb up into her room and comfort her.   145
But leave before they close the city gates,
For then you cannot get to Mantua,
Where you must live till we can find a time
To make your marriage known, to calm your kin,
To get the prince to pardon you, and call   150
You back with several million times more joy
Than what you had when you left here in grief—
Go now, nurse. Give your lady my respects
And have her hurry all the house to bed,
Which heavy sorrow makes them apt to do.   155
Romeo is coming.

NURSE
O Lord, I could have listened all night long
To such good guidance. O, what learnedness!
My lord, I'll tell my lady you will come.

ROMEO
And have my sweet arrange my punishment.   160

NURSE
Here, sir, a ring she said to give you, sir.

                    [She gives ROMEO a ring]

Go quick, make haste, for it grows very late.

[Exit]

ROMEO
My happiness is much revived by this!

FRIAR LAWRENCE
Go now, good night! Your situation's this:
Either be gone before they post the guards,   165
Or by the break of day leave in disguise
And stay in Mantua. I will find your servant,
And he will let you know from time to time
Of each improvement in your status here.
Give me your hand. It's late. Farewell. Good night.   170

ROMEO
If joy past joy did not call out so true,
I'd grieve to leave so hurriedly from you.
Farewell.

[Exit]

Scene Four. A Room in Capulet's House

[Enter CAPULET, LADY CAPULET,
and COUNTY PARIS]

CAPULET
Things have turned out, sir, so unfortunately
We've had no time to share this with our daughter.
You see, she loved her kinsman Tybalt dearly,
And so did I....Well, we were born to die.
It's very late. She won't come down tonight.   5
I have to say, if you had not come by,
I would have been in bed an hour ago.

COUNTY PARIS
This time of woe allows no time to woo.—
Good night. Give my regards, ma'am, to your daughter.

LADY CAPULET
I will, and get her thoughts on this tomorrow.   10
Tonight she's held beneath a heavy weight.

CAPULET
Sir Paris, somewhat recklessly, I pledge
My daughter's hand. I think she'll acquiesce
In all respects to me. It's done. Of course she will.—
Wife, go see her before you go to bed.   15
Inform her that my son-in-law's proposed
And tell her, get this right, on Wednesday next—
No, wait! What day is this?

COUNTY PARIS
                              Monday, my lord.

CAPULET
Monday! Hmmm. Well, then Wednesday is too soon.
We'll make it Thursday. Tell her that on Thursday   20
She will be married to this noble earl—
Will you be ready? Do you mind this haste?
Not much ado—a relative or two.
For, listen now, since Tybalt's just been killed
And is our kin, it may appear he's held   25
In low regard if there's too big a feast.
So we'll invite a half a dozen friends,
And leave it at that. How does Thursday sound?

COUNTY PARIS
My lord, I wish that Thursday were tomorrow.

CAPULET
Get going then—next Thursday it will be.   30
[to his wife] See Juliet now, before you go to bed,
And start preparing for this wedding day.—
Farewell, my lord.—Now take me to my room!—

My goodness, it's so very late that we
Can say it's early in a bit. Good night.   35

[Exit]

Scene Five. Juliet's Balcony, Above a Garden

[Enter ROMEO and JULIET]

JULIET
You wish to go? It still is not near day.
It was the nightingale, and not the lark,
That pierced the fretful hollow of your ear.
That pomegranate tree's her nightly perch.
Believe me, love, it was the nightingale.   5

ROMEO
It was the lark, the herald of the morn,
No nightingale. Look, love, malicious streaks,
They lace the clouds dispersing in the east.
Night's candles are burnt out, and jovial day
Stands tiptoe on the misty mountain tops.   10
I must be gone and live, or stay and die.

JULIET
That light is not daylight, I know it's so.
It is some meteor that the sun exhaled
To be for you tonight a torch-bearer
And lead you on your way to Mantua.   15
Stay longer then, you do not need to go.

ROMEO
Let me be seized, let me be put to death.
I am content, if you wish it to be.
I'll say that gray is not the morning's eye,
It's just the pale reflection of the moon.   20
And that's no lark whose notes reverb against

The arching sky so high above our heads.
The wish to stay exceeds the will to go.
Come, death, and welcome! Juliet wants it so.
How is my sweet? Let's talk? It is not day.   25

JULIET
It is, it is! Be quick, now go away!
It is the lark that sings so out of tune,
Discordant strains and jarring notes too sharp.
Some say the lark can intermingle tunes.
This one does not, for she's not mingling us.   30
Some say the lark and loathsome toad swap eyes.
I wish that they'd exchange their voices too,
For arm from arm we're scattered by the day.
"The Hunt is On", it calls, and you're away.
O, now be gone. More light and light it grows.   35

ROMEO
More light and light—then darker are our woes!

[Enter NURSE]

NURSE
Madam!

JULIET
Nurse?

NURSE
Your mother's up and coming to your chamber.
It's daylight now; be watchful, keep alert.   40

[Exit]

JULIET
Then, window, let day in, and let life out.

ROMEO
Farewell, farewell! One kiss, and I'll descend.

[Descends]

JULIET
Can you be gone? My lord, my husband, love!
I must hear from you every day and hour,
For in one minute there are many days.   45
Such counting means I will be rich in years
Before I once more see my Romeo!

ROMEO
Farewell!
I will neglect no opportunity
To find a way to send my love to thee.   50

JULIET
O, do you think we'll ever meet again?

ROMEO
I have no doubt, and all these woes will turn
To sweet remembrance in the time to come.

JULIET
O God! I have a soul that sees ill winds!
I seem to see you, now that you're below,   55
As one dead at the bottom of a tomb.
Either my eyesight's failed, or you look pale.

ROMEO
Believe me, love, in my eyes so do you.
Our sighs drink our blood dry. Adieu, adieu!

[Exit below]

JULIET
O fortune, fortune! All men say you're fickle.   60
But if that's so, what do you want with one
Renowned for faithfulness? Be fickle, fortune.
For then, I hope, you will not keep him long
But send him back.

LADY CAPULET
        [Within] Ho, daughter! Are you up?

JULIET
Who's that I hear? Could that still be my mother?   65
Could she be up so late, or down so early?
Oh, what unusual matter brings her here?

[Enter LADY CAPULET]

LADY CAPULET
How are you, Juliet?

JULIET
                    Madam, I am not well.

LADY CAPULET
Still mourning all this time your cousin's death?
You cannot wash him from his grave with tears,   70
And if you could, you could not make him live.
Enough. Some grief can show how much you love,
But too much always shows a lack of sense.

JULIET
Still I must mourn a loss that touched me so.

LADY CAPULET
You'll feel the touch of loss, but not the touch   75
Of loved ones mourned.

JULIET
                    And touched by such a loss,
Forever I must mourn for one so loved.

LADY CAPULET
Well, girl, it's not so much his death you mourn;
It's that the villain lives who murdered him.

JULIET
What villain, madam?

LADY CAPULET
                    Why that villain Romeo.   80

JULIET
Villain and he—they're miles apart by now.
May God forgive him! Said with all my heart,
Yet no man more than he has grieved my heart.

LADY CAPULET
That is because the murdering traitor lives.

JULIET
And far beyond the reach of these two hands.   85
Let them alone avenge my cousin's death!

LADY CAPULET
We'll get our vengeance on him, have no fear.
So weep no more. I'll tell someone in Mantua—
That's where this banished fugitive now lives—
To give him such an unexpected dose   90
That he will soon keep Tybalt company.
And then, I hope, you will be satisfied.

JULIET
Indeed I never will be satisfied
With Romeo till I behold him—dead—
Is my poor heart from pain for one so dear.   95
Madam, if you could simply find a man
To give the poison, I'd enhance the mix
So Romeo would, once he has taken it,
Soon sleep in peace. O, how my heart recoils
To hear his name—when I can't go to him   100
To hurl the love I had for cousin Tybalt
Upon the body that has murdered him!

LADY CAPULET
Prepare the means, and I'll find such a man.
But now you'll hear some joyful tidings, girl.

JULIET
And joy is welcome in this time of need.   105
What is this news, your ladyship, please say?

LADY CAPULET
Well, well, you have a caring father, child.
One who, to lift from you this heavy weight,
Arranged a day of joy that's soon to come,
One not foreseen by you, nor dreamed by me.   110

JULIET
Madam, how opportune, what day is this?

LADY CAPULET
Indeed, my child, early next Thursday morn
The gallant, young, and noble gentleman,
The County Paris, at St. Peter's Church
Will happily take you as his joyful bride.   115

JULIET
I swear by Peter's Church, and Peter too,
He shall not take me as his joyful bride.
I'm shocked that there's such haste that I must wed
Before my future husband's courted me.
I beg you, tell my lord and father, madam,   120
I will not marry yet, and when I do, I swear
I'd rather it were Romeo, whom you know
I hate, than Paris. This is news indeed!

LADY CAPULET
Here comes your father. Tell him this yourself,
And see how well he takes it from your mouth.   125

[Enter CAPULET and NURSE]

CAPULET
When the sun sets, the earth will drip with dew,
But with the sunset of my brother's son
It's full-on rain.
Good grief! A steady flow, girl. Still in tears?
Eternal showers? In one little body   130
You emulate a sailboat, sea and wind.
Your eyes, which I will take to be the sea,
Still ebb and flow with tears; your body is the boat,

Sailing in this salt flood; the winds, your sighs,
Which, raging with your tears, and all the rest   135
Unless a sudden calm descends, will swamp
Your tempest-tossed remains.—And you, my wife!
Have you delivered our decree to her?

LADY CAPULET
Yes, sir. She says "no thanks" to show her thanks.
For all I care, the fool can wed her grave!   140

CAPULET
Wait! Help me get this, help me get this, wife.
She says "No thanks." Is that how she says thanks?
Is she not proud? Does she not know she's blessed,
Unworthy as she is, that we've convinced
This worthy gentleman to marry her?   145

JULIET
Not proud you have, but thankful that you have.
I never will be proud of what I hate,
But thankful what I hate was meant as love.

CAPULET
What, what, who, how? Wrenched logic! What is this?
"Proud"—and "I thank you"—and "I thank you not"   150
And yet "not proud"—little Miss Monster, you,
Thank this not that, not proud this, not proud that.
Well, comb out your fine mane by Thursday girl,
And go with Paris to Saint Peter's Church,
Or I will drag you by the halter there.   155
Damn you, you bleached-out carcass! Worthless baggage!
You wax-faced…!

LADY CAPULET
                    [to CAPULET] Shame on you. Have you
          gone mad.²

JULIET
Good father, please, I beg you on my knees,
Be patient and allow me just one word.

CAPULET
Hang you, young baggage! Disobedient wretch!   160
I tell you what: be at that church on Thursday,
Or never look upon my face again.
Don't speak; do not reply; don't answer me.
My fingers itch.—We felt a bit denied,
When God had only blessed us with one child,   165
But now I see this one is one too much,
And that it was a curse to give us her.
To hell, you good-for-nothing!

NURSE
                              God help her!
It's shameful for my lord to scold her so.

CAPULET
Why's that, O Lady Wisdom? Hold your tongue,   170
Miss Prudence. Chatter with your gossips. Go.

NURSE
I meant no disobedience.

CAPULET
                          Enough.

NURSE
May one not speak?

CAPULET
                    Quiet, you babbling fool!
Share your deep thoughts with gossips over punch.
We do not need them here.

LADY CAPULET
                          You are too hot.   175

CAPULET
By God! This makes me mad. Day, night, work, play,
Alone, with others—always my concern

Has been to find a match, and that I have—
A gentleman of noble parentage,
A large estate, youthful, and nobly linked,   180
Equipped, as they might say, with attributes,
Proportioned as one's heart would wish a man—
And then to have a wretched, sniveling fool,
A whining doll who, when good fortune comes,
Replies, "I will not wed, I cannot love,   185
I am too young, now you must pardon me."
But, if you will not wed, I'll pardon you!
Graze where you wish, but you won't live with me.
Consider this. I am not one to jest.
Thursday is near. Speak to your heart and think.   190
If you are mine, I'll give you to my friend.
If not, then hang, beg, starve, die in the streets,
For, on my soul, I'll disinherit you,
And what is mine shall never go to you.
Don't doubt me. Think this through. I won't relent.   195

[Exit]

JULIET
Is there no pity sitting in the clouds,
That sees into the bottom of my grief?
Sweet mother, O, do not cast me away!
Delay this marriage for a month, a week,
Or, if you won't, then make a bridal bed   200
For me in that dark tomb where Tybalt lies.

LADY CAPULET
Don't talk to me, for I won't say a word.
Do as you wish, for I am through with you.

[Exit]

JULIET
O God! O nurse! How can this be prevented?
My husband's on this earth, my vow's with heaven.   205
How can that vow again be made on earth,
Unless my husband sends it back from heaven

By leaving earth? Comfort me, counsel me.
Why me? Why is it heaven plays such tricks
Upon so slight a target as myself!   210
Say something? Don't you have a word of hope?
Nurse, cheer me up.

NURSE
                          Well, here is how I see it.
Romeo is banished; and I'd bet the world
That he won't dare come back to stake his claim,
Or if he does, it better be by stealth.   215
The circumstances being as they stand,
I think it best you marry with the County.
O, he's a lovely gentleman!
Romeo's his dishrag. Why no eagle, madam,
Could have so clear, or quick or fine an eye   220
As Paris has. And curse this heart of mine,
If you aren't happy in this second match,
For it excels your first, and either way,
Your first is dead, or is as good as dead,
Since you live here and can't make use of him.   225

JULIET
Are these words from you heart?

NURSE
And from my soul. If not, then curse them both.

JULIET
Amen!

NURSE
What?

JULIET
A marvelous effort, nurse, to cheer me up.   230
Go out and tell my lady I have gone,
Having displeased my father, to Lawrence's cell,
To make confession and to be absolved.

NURSE
Indeed I will, for now you're making sense.

[Exit NURSE]

JULIET
Damn that old woman! What a wicked fiend!
Which sin is worse? To have me break my vow,   235
Or to disdain my lord with that same tongue
Which she had praised him with, beyond compare,
A thousand times before? Go, counselor.
You and my inner realm are now divorced.
I'll see what remedy the friar will try.   240
If all else fails, I'll have the means to die.

[Exit]

Romeo and Juliet

Act Four

Act Four

Scene One. Friar Lawrence's Cell

[Enter FRIAR LAWRENCE and COUNTY PARIS]

FRIAR LAWRENCE
On Thursday, sir? The time is very short.

COUNTY PARIS
My father-in-law Capulet insists;
And I am in no rush to slow him down.

FRIAR LAWRENCE
You say you do not know the lady's thoughts?
This course is roughly cut; I do not like it.   5

COUNTY PARIS
Without restraint she's mourning Tybalt's death,
And thus I've had no chance to talk of love;
A house of tears will not make Venus smile.
Now, sir, her father feels it's dangerous
That she allows her grief to rule her so,   10
And wisely pushes up our wedding day,
To stop the inundation of her tears,
Which, dwelled upon too much in solitude,
Perhaps are chased away by company.
Now you can see the reason for this haste.   15

FRIAR LAWRENCE
[Aside] I wish there were no reason not to rush.
[to COUNTY PARIS] Look, sir, the lady's coming toward
    my cell.

[Enter JULIET]

COUNTY PARIS
How fortunate, my lady and my wife!

JULIET
That may be, sir, since I may be a wife.

COUNTY PARIS
This Thursday, love, that "may" becomes a "must."   20

JULIET
What must be shall be.

FRIAR LAWRENCE
     That much we can trust.

COUNTY PARIS
You're here to make confession to this friar?

JULIET
To answer that, I must confess to you.

COUNTY PARIS
Do not deny to him that you love me.

JULIET
I will confess to you that I love him.   25

COUNTY PARIS
And you'll say, I am sure, that you love me.

JULIET
If I do so, it's value will be more,
If said behind your back than to your face.

COUNTY PARIS
Poor soul, your face is ravaged by these tears.

JULIET
Small victory for my tears in doing that,   30
For it was bad enough before their harm.

COUNTY PARIS
You hurt it more than tears do with that talk.

JULIET
It can't be slander, sir, if it's the truth,
And what I said, I said it to my face.

COUNTY PARIS
Your face is mine, and you have slandered it.   35

JULIET
That may be so, for it is not my own.
My holy father, are you busy now,
Or should I come to you at evening mass?

FRIAR LAWRENCE
I'm free to serve my saddened daughter, now.
My lord, we must request some time alone.   40

COUNTY PARIS
God help me if I interrupt devotion!
On early Thursday I will wake the bride.
Till then, adieu, and keep this holy kiss.

[Exit]

JULIET
O, shut the door, and when you have done that,
Come weep with me, past hope, past care, past help!   45

FRIAR LAWRENCE
Ah, Juliet, I already know your grief.
It strains me past the reach of all my wits.
I hear you will—and nothing can postpone it—
Be married Thursday morning to this County.

JULIET

Don't tell me, friar, that you've heard of this,   50
Unless you tell me how I may prevent it.
If, in your wisdom, you can give no help,
Then simply tell me my solution's wise,
And with this knife I'll give help instantly.
God joined my heart with Romeo's, you our hands;   55
Before this hand, whose seal you stamped on Romeo,
Can fix its seal upon another deed,
Or my true heart in treasonous revolt
Turns elsewhere, this must slay both hand and heart.
Therefore, turn to your long experience,   60
And give me guidance now, or else behold,
Between my plight and me, this bloody knife
Will be the umpire, arbitrating that
Which all the power of your years and skill
Could not bring to an honorable end.   65
Don't take too long to speak. I long to die,
Unless a remedy's in your reply.

FRIAR LAWRENCE

Wait, daughter. I still see a kind of hope,
One forcing action just as desperate
As this so desperate act we must prevent.   70
If, rather than to marry County Paris,
You have the strength of will to kill yourself,
Then it is likely you would undergo
A thing like death to cast away a shame
You wish to flee by suffering death itself.   75
If you will chance it, I'll supply the means.

JULIET

O, make me leap, rather than marry Paris,
Off of the battlements of that high tower,
Or walk where bandits lurk, or make me hide
Where serpents are. Chain me to roaring bears,   80
Or shut me every night in catacombs,
Submerge me under dead men's rattling bones,
With reeking limbs and yellow jawless skulls.

Or make me go into a new-made grave,
And hide me with a dead man in his shroud—   85
Things that, to hear them told, have made me tremble—
And I will do this without fear or doubt,
To stay an unstained wife to my sweet love.

FRIAR LAWRENCE
Wait, now. Go home, be cheerful, give consent
To marry Paris. Wednesday is tomorrow.   90
Tomorrow night see that you sleep alone,
Don't let your nurse sleep with you in your chamber.
Take home this vial, and when you are in bed,
Drink all this quickly-working liquid down,
Which, instantly, will send through all your veins   95
A cold and drowsy feeling, and your pulse
Will slow its natural rhythm and then cease.
No warmth, no breath will indicate you're living.
The roses in your lips and cheeks will fade
To whitish ash, your eyes will draw their shades,   100
Like death, when it shuts down the day of life.
Each part, deprived of flexibility,
Now barren, stiff, and cold, will look like death,
And in this borrowed state of shrunken death
You will remain for forty hours or so,   105
And then awake as if from pleasant sleep.
Now, when the bridegroom in the morning comes
To rouse you from your bed, you'll be there dead.
Then, as the customs of our land demand,
In your best robes, and bare-faced, on the bier,   110
You will be carried to the ancient vault
Where all departed Capulets are placed.
Meanwhile, so he'll be there when you awake,
I'll write to Romeo telling him our plan.
And he'll come here, and then both he and I   115
Will wait for you to wake, and that same night
He'll transport you from here to Mantua.
And this will free you from this present shame,
If no erratic whim or girlish fear
Depletes the courage to go through with this.   120

JULIET
Give it, give it! Don't talk to me of fear!

FRIAR LAWRENCE
Wait. Go on home. Be strong and prosperous
In this endeavor. I will rush a friar
To Mantua, with my letter to your lord.

JULIET
Love give me strength and help that strength affords.   125
Farewell, dear father.

[Exit]

Scene Two. Hall in Capulet's House

[Enter CAPULET, LADY CAPULET,
NURSE, and SERVANTS]

CAPULET
Invite whatever guests are on this list.

[Exit first SERVANT]

You there, go hire me twenty skillful cooks.

2ND SERVANT
There won't be any bad ones, sir, for I'll make sure they
taste their fingers.

CAPULET
What purpose would that have?   5

2ND SERVANT
Truly, sir, it's a bad sign when a cook won't taste his own
fingers: so he who will not lick his fingers will not come
with me.

CAPULET
Go, get on with it.

[Exit second SERVANT]

This time we will be very unprepared.   10
And...has my daughter gone to Friar Lawrence?

NURSE
Ay, that she did.

CAPULET
Let's hope he has some good effect on her.
A mulish self-willed waywardness it is.

NURSE
Look she's come back, and with a cheerful look.   15

[Enter JULIET]

CAPULET
My headstrong one! And where have you been dawdling?

JULIET
Where I have learned how to repent the sin
Of disobedient opposition both
To you and your commands, and have been told
By Friar Lawrence to fall prostrate here [kneeling]   20
And beg forgiveness. Please forgive me, father.
From now on I'm forever ruled by you.

CAPULET
Send for the County. Tell him of all this.
I'll have this knot tied up tomorrow morning.

JULIET
I met the youthful lord at Lawrence' cell.   25
And gave to him what love seemed suitable,
Kept well within the bounds of modesty.

CAPULET
I'm glad of that. Yes, this is good—stand up—
Just as it should be. Let me see the County.
Yes, that's it, go, I say, and bring him here.   30
And now, by God, this reverend holy friar,
All of our city is in debt to him.

JULIET
Nurse, will you come with me into my room,
To help me pick appropriate attire
Which, in your view, is fit to wear tomorrow?   35

LADY CAPULET
No, not till Thursday. There is time enough.

CAPULET
Nurse, go with her. We go to church tomorrow.

[Exit JULIET and NURSE]

LADY CAPULET
We'll have to cut the preparations short.
It's almost dark.

CAPULET
                    Tut, I'll get busy now,
And it will all work out. Just trust me, wife.   40
You go to Juliet, help to deck her out.
I'll stay up all night long—leave this to me—
I'll be the housewife just this once.—What, ho!—
They are all out. Well, I will walk myself
To County Paris, and I'll set him straight   45
About tomorrow. My heart is strangely light
Now that this wayward girl has been reclaimed.

[Exit]

Scene Three. Juliet's Chamber

[Enter JULIET and NURSE]

JULIET
Yes, that attire is best. But, gentle nurse,
I ask that I be left alone tonight,
For heaven will need many prayers from me
To smile upon my state, which you well know
Is full of sin and runs against its will.   5

[Enter LADY CAPULET]

LADY CAPULET
Still busy here? Can I be of some help?

JULIET
No, madam, we have picked out all the things
Tomorrow's ceremony would require.
So if you please, I wish to be alone.
Perhaps the nurse can stay with you tonight,   10
For I am sure your hands are much too full
With all this sudden business.

LADY CAPULET
                              Then good night.
Now get in bed, and get the rest you need.

[Exit LADY CAPULET and NURSE]

JULIET
Farewell!—God knows when we will meet again.
A cold and dizzy fear thrills through my veins   15
And almost freezes up the heat of life.
I'll call them back again to comfort me.
Nurse!—What could she do here?
This ghastly scene I need to act alone.
The vial.   20

[takes out the vial]

What if this potion does not work at all?
Will I be married, then, tomorrow morning?
No, No! This will prevent it.

[She takes out a dagger and lays it beside her]

                     —Stay right there.
What if this is a poison, which the friar
Has cunningly dispensed to make me die,   25
To keep this marriage from disgracing him,
Because he married me before to Romeo?
I fear it is, and yet I sense it's not,
For he has always proved a holy man.[1]
What if, when I am placed into the tomb,   30
I wake before the time that Romeo
Comes to redeem me? That's a fearful thought!
And won't I lie there gasping in the vault,
Whose foul mouth never breathes in wholesome air,
And suffocate before my Romeo comes?   35
Or, if I live, is it not likely that
This horrible display of death and night,
Together with the terror of the place,
There in a vault, an ancient storage place,
Where, for so many centuries, the bones   40
Of all my buried ancestors are packed;
Where bloody Tybalt, freshly green in death,
Lies festering in his shroud; where, as they say,
At some late hour at night the spirits meet—
O lord, o lord, is it not likely that,   45
I'll wake too soon—among the loathsome smells
And shrieks of roots torn from the earth above
That make the mortals hearing them run mad—
O, if I wake, won't I become distraught,
Encircled there with all these hideous fears,   50
Insanely play with my forefathers' teeth,
And pluck the mangled Tybalt from his shroud,
And, in a frenzy, with some kinsman's bone,
To be my club, dash out my desperate brains?
O, look! I think I see my cousin's ghost   55

Seeking out Romeo, who impaled his body
Upon a rapier's point. Stop, Tybalt, stop!
Romeo, I'm coming. This I drink to you.

[JULIET drinks and falls upon her bed behind curtains]

Scene Four. A Hall in Capulet's House

[Enter LADY CAPULET and NURSE]

LADY CAPULET
Here, take these keys and fetch more spices, nurse.

NURSE
They need more dates and berries for the pastries.

[Enter CAPULET]

CAPULET
Let's go! Let's go. The chime just rang three times.
The curfew bell has rung, it's three o'clock.—
Go check the pastries, dear Angelica.   5
Spare no expense.

NURSE
                              Now go, you kitchen-nag.
You get to bed, or you'll be sick to-morrow
From dogging us all night.

CAPULET
No, not a chance. Why, I have dogged all night
And for a lesser cause and not been sick.   10

LADY CAPULET
Yes, you have chased a cat or two at times,
But I will dog you if you dog them now.

[Exit LADY CAPULET and NURSE]

CAPULET
I sense a jealous bone!

[Enter SERVANTS, with spits, logs and baskets]

Now, tell me fellow,
What is this?

1ST SERVANT
Things for the cook, sir, but I don't know what.   15

CAPULET
Then hurry.

[Exit 1ST SERVANT]

—You, go split some drier logs.
Have Peter take you to the chopping block.

2ND SERVANT
This splitting head's already on the block.
Don't bother troubling Peter with this matter.

[Exit]

CAPULET
Well-put, indeed. A merry bastard, ha!   20
A blockhead's what you are.—Good lord, it's light.
The County will be here with music soon,
Just as he said he would.

[Music within]

I hear them now.
Nurse!—Wife!—Come here!—O, nurse, I say!

[Re-enter NURSE]

Go, wake up Juliet. Go and get her dressed.   25
I'll go and chat with Paris. Go, be quick.
Be quick! The bridegroom is already here.
Be quick, I say.

[Exit]

Scene Five. Juliet's Chamber; Juliet on the Bed

[Enter NURSE]

NURSE
Mistress! O, mistress! Juliet!—Fast asleep, I bet.
Why, lamb! Why, lady!—Sleeping like a slug!
Why, love, I say! Madam! Sweetheart! Why, bride!
What, not a word? You've had your penny's worth.
Sleep for a week, for by tonight, I tell you,   5
The County, rest assured, will stack the deck
And you'll rest little.—God forgive my tongue!
The blesséd Virgin, how sound asleep she is!
I have to wake her.—Madam, madam, madam!
The county can't get hitched to you in bed,   10
Though that would fill your wagon. Won't she rise?
What, dressed and in your clothes, and down again!
I have to wake you. Lady, lady, lady!—
O lord, o lord! Help, help! My lady's dead!
O, curse the very day that I was born!   15
Some brandy, please. O god! My lord! My lady!

[Enter LADY CAPULET]

LADY CAPULET
What's all this noise?

NURSE
                    O lord, a mournful day!

LADY CAPULET
What is the matter?

NURSE
                    Look, look! A dreadful day!

LADY CAPULET
O my, O my! My child, my only life!
Revive, look up, or I will die with you!   20
Help, help! Get help.

                    [Enter CAPULET]

CAPULET
Honestly, where is she? Her lord is here.

NURSE
She's dead, deceased, she's dead. O, curse this day!

LADY CAPULET
O curse this day, she's dead, she's dead, she's dead!

CAPULET
Ha! Let me look at her. My God, she's cold.   25
Her blood has settled, and her joints are stiff.
Life and these lips have long been separated.
Death lies on her just like an early frost
Upon the sweetest flower in all the field.

NURSE
A mournful day!

LADY CAPULET
                    O, what a woeful time!   30

CAPULET
Death, which has married her to make me wail,
Ties up my tongue and will not let me speak.

[Enter FRIAR LAWRENCE and
COUNTY PARIS, with MUSICIANS]

FRIAR LAWRENCE
Well, is the bride ready to go to church?

CAPULET
Ready to go, but never to return.—
O son, the night before your wedding day   35
Your bride has lain with death. There she lies,
The flower that she was, deflowered by him.
Death is my son-in-law, death is my heir.
My daughter he has wedded. I will die
And leave it all. Life, living, all to death.   40

COUNTY PARIS
Is this the face that I have longed to see,[2]
And could it give me such a sight as this?

LADY CAPULET
Accursed, disastrous, wretched, hateful day!
Most miserable hour that time has seen
In its unceasing, toilsome pilgrimage!   45
Just one, poor one, one poor and loving child,
Just one thing to enjoy and celebrate,
And cruel death has snatched it from my sight!

NURSE
O pain! O painful, painful, painful day!
Most mournful of all days, most painful day   50
That I have ever, ever had to see!
O day! O day! O day! O hateful day!
There never was a day as black as this:
O painful day! O painful day!

COUNTY PARIS
Betrayed, divorced from, wronged and spited, slain!   55
Abominable death, betrayed by you,
By cruel cruel you, completely overthrown!
O love! O life! Not life, but love in death!

CAPULET
Despised, distressed, and hated, martyred, killed!
Discomforting event, why happen now   60
To murder, murder our festivities?
O child! O child! My soul, and not my child!
Dead you are! O lord, my child is dead,
And with my child my joys are buried too!

FRIAR LAWRENCE
Shame on this noise! Calamity's not cured   65
By such commotion. Heaven and you all
Have shared this maiden. Heaven now takes all,
And that is all the better for this girl.
The part you share could not be kept from death,
But heaven gives its part eternal life.   70
The most you sought for her was gain in wealth,
Your heaven was to help her raise her rank,
So why weep now, when she is being raised
Above the clouds, as high as heaven itself?
You mourn your child with love so ill-at-ease   75
That you go mad when she is finding peace.
Her marriage is not good because its long.
But she's best married that dies married young.
Dry up your tears, and pin your memories
To this dear body, and, as custom says,   80
In all her best array bring her to church.
For though our foolish nature's drawn to grief,
Still nature's tears are reason for relief.

CAPULET
The things intended for a festival,
Transform them to a somber funeral: 85
Our instruments to melancholy bells,
Our wedding feast to a sad burial meal,
Our joyous hymns to mournful elegies,
Our bridal flowers will decorate the grave,
And all these other things must likewise change.   90

FRIAR LAWRENCE
Sir, go on in, and, madam, go with him,

And go, Sir Paris. Everyone prepare
To usher this fair maiden to her grave.
It seems you angered heaven with ill deeds.
It frowns upon defiance of its creeds.   95

      [Exit CAPULET, LADY CAPULET, COUNTY
            PARIS, and FRIAR LAWRENCE]

1ST MUSICIAN
This means we can pack our pipes and leave.

NURSE
Honest good fellows, ah, pack up, pack up,
For you well know this is a pitiful case.

            [Exit]

1ST MUSICIAN
In my case, though, the case can be repaired. [indicating
his instrument case]

           [Enter PETER]

PETER
Musicians, O, musicians, play the tune "Heart's Ease," 100
"Heart's Ease." If you want me to live, play "Heart's Ease."

1ST MUSICIAN
Why "Heart's Ease"?

PETER
O, musicians, because my heart's already playing "My
Heart is Filled with Pain." O, cheer me up with some sad
song.   105

1ST MUSICIAN
We're not much for sad songs. Now's not the time.

PETER
You won't play it then?

1ST MUSICIAN
No.

PETER
Then I will give you something to sing about.

1ST MUSICIAN
What will you give us?   110

PETER
Not money, that's for sure—but I'll razz you. I will call you
"choir boy."

1ST MUSICIAN
Then you must be the creature who folds my robe.

PETER
And I will lay this creature's dagger across your noggin. I
won't dance to your tune [jabbing with his dagger]. I'll "do- 115
re-me" you. I'll even "fa" you. Are you noting this?

1ST MUSICIAN
If you "do" us and "re" us, then you are noting us.

2ND MUSICIAN
Please pack up your dagger, and unpack your brain.

PETER
Then I'll go at you with my brain! I will slap you silly with
this brain of iron and put away my iron dagger. Answer 120
me like men: [sings]
    "When gripped with grief the heart's oppressed,
      And in the dumps the mind's depressed,
    Then music with her silver sound"—
Why "silver sound"? Why "music with her silver sound"? 125
What do you say, Simon Stringplucker?

1ST MUSICIAN
No doubt, sir, it's because silver has a sweet sound.

PETER
Cute! What do you say, Hugh Fiddlescratcher?

2ᴺᴰ MUSICIAN
I say "silver sound" because musicians play for silver.

PETER
Cute again! What do say you, James Soundhole? 130

3ᴿᴰ MUSICIAN
Truly, I don't know what to say.

PETER
Then if I may. You're just a singer, so I will speak for you. It
is "music with her silver sound" because musicians wouldn't
know the sound of gold: [sings]
"Then music with her silver sound 135
Lends speedy help to bring us round."

[Exit]

1ˢᵀ MUSICIAN
What an annoying pest he is!

2ᴺᴰ MUSICIAN
Hang him, Jack! Come on, we'll go in here, mingle with the
mourners, and grab us some dinner.

[Exit]

Romeo and Juliet

Act Five

Act Five

Scene One. Mantua. A Street

[Enter ROMEO]

ROMEO
If I can trust the rosy "truth" of sleep,
My dreams foretell of joyful news at hand.
My bosom's king sits lightly on his throne,
And all this day an unaccustomed spirit
Lifts me above the ground with cheerful thoughts.   5
I dreamt my lady came and found me dead,
Strange dream that gave a dead man leave to think!
And kisses breathed such life into my lips,
That I revived, and was an emperor.
Oh my! The sweetness that love must possess,   10
When shimmers of it are so rich in joy!

[Enter BALTHAZAR]

News from Verona!—Welcome, Balthazar.
Do you have letters for me from the friar?
How is my lady? Is my father well?
How is my Juliet? I asked that twice,   15
For nothing can be ill if she is well.

BALTHAZAR (servant of Romeo)
Then she is well, and nothing can be ill.
Her body's in the Capulet's family tomb,
And her immortal part's with angels now.
I saw her laid down in her kindred's vault,   20
And instantly rode here to tell you this.

O, pardon me for bringing such bad news,
But you did say it was my duty, sir.

ROMEO
Could this be true? Then I defy you, stars!—
You know my home. Go get me ink and paper,   25
And hire some horses. I'll go there tonight.

BALTHAZAR
I beg you, sir, please show some self-control.
You look so pale and wild, and seem steered toward
Some great disaster.

ROMEO
                            Tut, you've got it wrong.
Leave me, and do the things I asked you to.   30
Don't you have letters to me from the friar?

BALTHAZAR
No, my good lord.

ROMEO
                          No matter. Now be off,
And hire those horses. I'll be with you soon.

                    [Exit BALTHAZAR]

Well, Juliet, I will lie with you tonight.
I'll find a way. O trouble, you are quick   35
To enter in the thoughts of desperate men!
I do remember an old herbalist,
Who lives nearby, whom recently I saw
In tattered clothes, with overhanging brow,
Collecting herbs. Impoverished he appeared,   40
Sharp misery had worn him to the bone.
And in his paltry shop a tortoise hung,
An alligator, stuffed, and other skins
Of odd-shaped fish; and strewn about his shelves
A sparse collection of some empty boxes,   45

Green earthen pots, bladders, and musty seeds,
Remnants of packing twine, and used-up petals
Were thinly scattered, making a display.
Noting this poverty, I told myself,
That if a man had need of poison now,   50
Though selling it means death in Mantua,
I still could buy it from this wretched soul.
This thought anticipates my current need.
And this same paltry man must sell me some.
If I remember, this should be his house.   55
A holiday, the beggar's shop is closed.—
Ho! Herbalist!

                    [Enter HERBALIST]

HERBALIST
Who yells so loud?

ROMEO
Come here, my man. I see that you are poor.
Wait, here are forty ducats. [Hands him gold coins] Let
    me have   60
A dram of poison, a fast-acting one
That spreads itself through all the taker's veins
So the life-weary soul will fall down dead,
Expelling from his body all his breath
As violent as a blast of powder fired   65
From deep within a deadly cannon's womb.

HERBALIST
Such mortal drugs I have, but Mantua's law
Means death for any man caught selling them.

ROMEO
You're threadbare now and full of wretchedness
And apt to die. And famine's in your cheeks,   70
Oppressive hardship's starving in your eyes,
Disgrace of begging hangs upon your back,
The world is not your friend, nor is it's law.

The world provides no law to make you rich.
So don't be poor, but break it and take this.   75

HERBALIST
My poverty consents; my conscience won't.

ROMEO
To poverty, not conscience I appeal.

HERBALIST
Mix this in any liquid that you wish,
And drink it down; and if you had the strength
Of twenty men, you still would go down quick.   80

ROMEO
Here is your gold, worse poison to men's souls,
Doing more murder in this loathsome world
Than these poor potions that you may not sell.
I've sold you poison; you have sold me none.
Farewell, buy food and put some flesh on you.   85

[HERBALIST exits]

Come with me—not to poison but renew—
To Juliet's grave, for there I must use you.

[Exit]

Scene Two. Friar Lawrence's Cell

[Enter FRIAR JOHN]

FRIAR JOHN
Holy Franciscan friar! Brother, ho!

[Enter FRIAR LAWRENCE]

FRIAR LAWRENCE
This voice no doubt belongs to Friar John.
Welcome from Mantua. What does Romeo say?
Or, if he wrote it down, give me his letter.

FRIAR JOHN
[speaking hurriedly] Out looking for a fellow barefoot
    brother,   5
One from our order, to accompany me,
Here in this city visiting the sick,
I found him, but the town's plague officers,
Suspecting that we both were in a house
Where the infectious pestilence had spread,   10
They quarantined us, would not let us leave,
And so I never got to Mantua.

FRIAR LAWRENCE
Who took my letter, then, to Romeo?

FRIAR JOHN
I couldn't send it to him—here it is—
Or send it back to you by messenger,   15
Because they're so afraid of the infection.

FRIAR LAWRENCE
Disastrous luck! I swear upon these robes,
That letter's critical, and full of news
Of great importance, and neglecting it
May do much harm. Go, Friar John, go quick   20
And bring an iron crowbar to me here,
Here to my cell.

FRIAR JOHN
                    Brother, I'll go and bring it here.

                        [Exit]

FRIAR LAWRENCE
I must go to the Capulet's vault alone.
Within three hours Juliet will awake.

She'll lay great blame on me that Romeo   25
Has not been kept informed of these events,
But first I'll write again to Mantua.
Till Romeo comes I'll keep her in my room.
Poor living corpse, closed in a dead man's tomb!

[Exit]

Scene Three. Churchyard near the Capulet Vault

[Enter COUNTY PARIS and his PAGE,
bearing flowers and a torch]

COUNTY PARIS
Give me your torch, boy. Go, and stand aside.
Best put it out; I don't wish to be seen.
Under that yew tree lay yourself down flat,
Holding your ear close to the churchyard ground
So hollowed-out, so loose, and so unfirm   5
From digging all these graves, no foot can step
Or you would hear it. Whistle out to me,
To signal that you hear someone approach.
Give me those flowers. Do what I tell you. Go.

PAGE (to Paris)
[Aside] I'm almost too afraid to be alone   10
Here in the churchyard. But I'll take my chances.

[Withdraws. PARIS tosses flowers
around the churchyard]

COUNTY PARIS
Sweet flower, your bridal bed's graced with this flower—
    O woe! Your canopy is dust and stones!—
Which I will spray with scented mist each hour,
    Or, if without, with tears distilled from moans.   15
The tokens of your memory that I keep,

Each night I'll toss upon your grave and weep.

[The PAGE whistles]

He's warning me that someone's coming near.
What curséd foot would wander here so late,
To spoil my loving tribute to my mate?   20
What, with a torch! Night, you can lend me cover.

[COUNTY PARIS withdraws]
[Enter ROMEO and BALTHAZAR
with a torch and tools]

ROMEO
Give me that mattock and the crowbar there.
Wait, take this letter. Early in the morning
See it's delivered to my lord and father.
Give me the light, and swear on pain of death,   25
Whatever you might hear or see stand back,
Do not attempt to interfere with me.
Why I'll descend into this bed of death
Is partly to behold my lady's face,
But chiefly to remove from her dead finger   30
A precious ring, a ring that has for me
A vital purpose. Therefore go, be gone.
But if suspicion brings you back to pry
Into what else I might intend to do,
By heaven, I will tear you joint from joint,   35
And deck this hungry churchyard with your limbs.
The time and my intent are savage-wild,
More fierce and more implacable by far
Than famished tigers or the roaring sea.

BALTHAZAR
I will be off, sir, and not trouble you.   40

ROMEO
Then you have shown your friendship. Here take this.
Live, and be prosperous. And farewell, good fellow.

BALTHAZAR
[aside] But all the same, I'll hide just out of sight.
His look and frame of mind do not seem right.

[BALTHAZAR withdraws]

ROMEO
You vile, repugnant jaws, you bowels of death,   45
Gorged with the dearest morsel of the earth,
And so I force your rotten jaws to open,

[Breaking open the door of the monument]

And out of spite, I'll cram you with more food!

COUNTY PARIS
This is that banished haughty Montague
Who murdered my love's kin, and grief for him,   50
It is supposed, caused this fair creature's death,
And now he's here to do some perverse harm
To their dead bodies. I will apprehend him.

[Advances toward ROMEO]

Stop your unholy toil, vile Montague!
Can vengeance be pursued beyond the grave?   55
Convicted villain, I hereby arrest you.
Obey, and come with me, for you must die.

ROMEO
I must indeed, and therefore I came here.
Good gentle youth, don't tempt a desperate man.
Flee now and leave me. Think of those now gone,   60
And let them frighten you. I beg you, youth.
Don't place another sin upon my head
By driving me to fury. O, be gone!
By heaven, I love you more than myself,
For I have come here armed against myself.   65
Don't stay, be gone now. Live, and henceforth say,
A madman's mercy begged me run away.

COUNTY PARIS
I must defy your self-denouncing plea,
And apprehend you as a felon now.

ROMEO
If you want to provoke me boy, take this!   70

[They fight]

PAGE
O lord, they're fighting! I'll go call the guards.

[Exit]

COUNTY PARIS
O, I am slain!

[Falls]

If you are merciful,
Open the tomb; lay me with Juliet.

[Dies]

ROMEO
I swear, I will. Let me peruse this face.
Mercutio's kinsman, noble County Paris!   75
What words were those, when my unsettled soul
Ignored my servant as we rode? I think
He told me Paris was to marry Juliet.
Weren't those his words? Or did I dream it up?
Or so disturbed when Paris spoke of Juliet   80
That I assumed it?—O, give me your hand;
We're entered now in sad misfortune's book!
I'll rest your body in a splendid grave.
A grave? No, a glass tower, slaughtered youth,
For here lies Juliet, whose beauty makes   85
This vault a festive palace full of light.
Death, laid to rest, by one already dead.

[Opening the tomb and laying PARIS in it]

How often when they're at the point of death
Have men felt cheerful, which their nurses call
The lift that precedes death. O, how can I   90
Call this a lifting?—O my love, my wife!
Death, which has sucked the honey from your breath,
Has yet to use its power on your beauty.
You are not conquered. Beauty's colors still
Fly crimson in your lips and in your cheeks,   95
And death's pale flag has not been raised there yet.—
Tybalt, are you beneath that bloody shroud?
What greater favor can I do for you
Than take the hand that cut your youth in two
And sever his who was your enemy?   100
Forgive me, cousin!—Ah, dear Juliet,
Are you so lovely still? Should I conclude
That immaterial death is fond of love,
And that this lean, abhorrent monster hides
You in the dark to be his paramour?   105
For fear of that I'll always stay with you,
And never from this palace of dim night
Depart again. Here, here I will remain
With worms that are your chambermaids. O, here
Is where I'll choose to find eternal rest,   110
And lift the yoke of inauspicious stars
From this world-weary flesh.—Eyes, one last look!
Arms, take your last embrace. And, lips, O you
The doors of breath, seal with a legal kiss
An open and exclusive deal with death.   115
Come, bitter escort, come, unsavory guide!
You reckless pilot, run at once upon
The dashing rocks your ocean-weary craft!
Here's to my love!

[Drinks]

The herbalist did not lie.
Your drugs are quick. Thus with a kiss I die.   120

[ROMEO dies]
[Enter, at the other end of the Churchyard, FRIAR
LAWRENCE, with a lantern, crowbar, and spade]

FRIAR LAWRENCE
Saint Francis help me! These old feet tonight
Have stumbled over many graves! Who's there?

BALTHAZAR
Just me, a friend, and one who knows you well.

FRIAR LAWRENCE
May heaven bless you! Tell me, my good friend,
What torch is this that lends its light in vain   125
To grubs and eyeless skulls? It looks as if
It's burning in the Capulet family vault.

BALTHAZAR
It is, o holy sir, and there's my master,
One that you love.

FRIAR LAWRENCE
                    Who is it?

BALTHAZAR
                         Romeo.

FRIAR LAWRENCE
How long has he been there?

BALTHAZAR
                              A good half hour.   130

FRIAR LAWRENCE
Come with me to the vault.

BALTHAZAR
                          I'd rather not, sir.
My master thinks that I have left from here,

And terrified me with the threat of death
If I stayed here to check on his intent.

FRIAR LAWRENCE
Wait then, I'll go alone. My fear is growing.   135
I deeply fear some evil, harmful thing.

BALTHAZAR
As I dozed off under this yew tree here,
I dreamt my master and another fought,
And that my master slew him.

FRIAR LAWRENCE
                              Romeo!

[Stoops and looks at the blood and weapons]

Oh, no. Oh, no! Whose blood is this that stains   140
The stony entrance of this sepulcher?
Why did their owners leave these gory swords
To lie discolored near this place of peace?

[Enters the vault]

Romeo! O, pale! Who else? What, Paris too?
And steeped in blood? How could one aberrant hour   145
Be guilty of such sorrowful events!
The lady's stirring.

[JULIET wakes and stirs]

JULIET
O comfort-giving friar! Where is my lord?
I still remember well where I should be,
And here I am. Where is my Romeo?   150

[Noise within]

FRIAR LAWRENCE
I hear some noise. Lady, let's leave this nest

Of death, contagion, and unnatural sleep.
A greater power than we can contradict
Has thwarted our intent. Come, come away!
Your husband's lying dead here in your lap,   155
And Paris too. I'll take you now to live
Among a sisterhood of holy nuns.
No time for questions, for the guard is coming.
Come, go, dear Juliet.

[noise within]

It's dangerous for me here.

JULIET
Go, go from here, for I will not depart.   160

[Exit FRIAR LAWRENCE]

What's this? A cup, held in my true love's hand?
Poison, I see, was his untimely end.
You sneak! All gone, and not one drop to share
To help me follow? I will kiss your lips.
Perhaps some poison drops still cling to them,   165
To make me die and thus make me restored.

[Kisses him]

Your lips are warm!

[enter the PAGE and GUARDS]

1ST GUARD
Lead, boy, which way?

JULIET
Huh, noise? Then I'll be quick. What luck, a dagger!

[Snatching ROMEO's dagger]

Make this your sheath.

[JULIET stabs herself in the chest]

Rust there, and let me die.   170

[JULIET falls on ROMEO's body and dies]

[Enter more GUARDS, with Paris' PAGE]

PAGE
This is the place; there, where the torch is burning.

1ST GUARD
The ground is bloody. Search around the churchyard.
Go, some of you, arrest whoever's here.

[Exit some of the GUARD]

Pitiful sight! The county's body's here.
And Juliet's bleeding, warm, and not dead long,   175
Though she was laid here several days ago.—
Go, tell the prince. Run to the Capulets.
Wake up the Montagues. You others search.

[Exit the rest of the GUARD]

We see the ground on which these sorrows lie,
And wish to know the grounds for such sad deeds,   180
But cannot without details fathom why.

[Re-enter some of the GUARD with BALTHAZAR]

2ND GUARD
Here's Romeo's servant. He was in the churchyard.

1ST GUARD
Hold onto him until the prince arrives.

[Re-enter the rest of the GUARD
with FRIAR LAWRENCE]

3ᴿᴰ GUARD
We found this trembling, sighing, weeping friar.
We took this mattock and this spade from him   185
As he was leaving from the churchyard there.

1ˢᵀ GUARD
Cause for suspicion. Hold the friar too.

[Enter PRINCE ESCALUS and ATTENDANTS]

PRINCE ESCALUS
Now what disaster's up so early here
That you must rouse your leader from his sleep?

[Enter CAPULET, LADY CAPULET, and others]

CAPULET
What's causing all this screaming in the streets?   190

LADY CAPULET
I hear the people crying "Romeo,"
Some "Juliet", and some "Paris," while they run
In such an uproar toward our family tomb.

PRINCE ESCALUS
What dreadfulness here sounds with such a start?

1ˢᵀ GUARD
Sovereign, the County Paris lies here slain,   195
Here's Romeo dead, here's Juliet, dead before,
But warmed and killed again.

PRINCE ESCALUS
Search, seek, and learn how these foul deeds occurred.

1ˢᵀ GUARD
Here is a friar, and slaughtered Romeo's servant
Equipped with all the tools they need to open   200
These dead men's tombs.

CAPULET
O heavens! O wife, look how our daughter bleeds!
This dagger went awry, for look, it's case
Is empty on the back of Montague,
And wrongly sheathed now in my daughter's bosom!   205

LADY CAPULET
O my! This sight of death is like a bell
That leads my old age to a sepulcher.

[Enter MONTAGUE and others]

PRINCE ESCALUS
Come, Montague. You're up before your time
To see your son and heir down much too soon.

MONTAGUE
Alas, my liege, my wife has died tonight.   210
Her grief from my son's exile stopped her breath.
What further woe conspires against my age?

PRINCE ESCALUS
Look, and you will see.

MONTAGUE
O you unmannered youth! Who taught you this,
To crowd past your own father to a grave?   215

PRINCE ESCALUS
Seal up the mouth of outrage for a while,
Till we are clear of all uncertainty,
And know the source, the flow, and its true course,
And then I'll take command of all your grief,
If it means taking lives. For now, refrain,   220
And let calm be the master of misfortune.
So now bring all suspicious parties forth.

FRIAR LAWRENCE
I top the list, the one least capable,
Yet since the time and place both point to me,

I'm most suspected of these dismal murders.   225
And here I stand, both to accuse and clear,
To see myself acquitted and condemned.

PRINCE ESCALUS
Then tell at once all that you know of this.

FRIAR LAWRENCE
I will be brief, for my short date with life
Now lacks the breath to tell this tedious tale.   230
Romeo, now dead, had married Juliet,
And she, now dead, was Romeo's faithful wife.
I wed them, and their secret wedding day
Was Tybalt's doomsday, whose untimely death
Banished the just-wed bridegroom from this city,   235
For whom, and not for Tybalt, Juliet pined.
To lift the siege of grief surrounding her,
You pledged and would have married her by force
To County Paris. Then she came to me,
And with wild looks, told me to find some means   240
To free her somehow from this second marriage,
Or right there in my cell she'd kill herself.
I gave her, being tutored in such arts,
A sleeping potion, one which took effect
As I intended, and produced in her   245
The look of death. Meanwhile, I wrote to Romeo
And told him to come here this dreadful night,
To help to take her from her borrowed grave,
Just at the time the potion would wear off.
But Friar John, through whom I sent the note,   250
Was stopped by chance events and forced last night
To hand the letter back. Then all alone,
The preset hour for her to wake now near,
I came to take her from her family's vault,
Meaning to keep her hidden in my cell   255
Until the time was right to contact Romeo.
But when I got here, right about the time
She would come to, here in untimely death
Lay noble Paris and true Romeo.

She then woke up, and I asked her to come   260
And calmly bear what heaven's will has done.
Then frightened by a noise I left the tomb,
But she, in such despair, refused to leave
And, it appears, did violence to herself.
All this I know alone; as for the marriage   265
Her nurse was privy to it. If anything
Was harmed by my misdeeds, let my old life
Be sacrificed, an hour or so too soon,
By rigorous application of harsh law.

PRINCE ESCALUS
We've always known you as a holy man.—   270
Where's Romeo's servant? What has he to say?

BALTHAZAR
I brought my master news of Juliet's death,
And then in haste he came from Mantua
Right to this place, right to this catacomb,
Says give this note this morning to his father,   275
And threatens me with death if I attempt
To follow after him into the vault.

PRINCE ESCALUS
Give me the note, I want to look at it.
Where is the County's page who called the guard?
You boy, what brought your master to this place?   280

PAGE
He came with flowers for his lady's grave,
And said to keep my distance, so I did.
Then someone with a light breaks in the tomb,
And right away my master draws on him,
And then I ran away to call the guard.   285

PRINCE ESCALUS
This note corroborates the friar's words,
The course their love took, tidings of her death,
And here he writes about him buying poison

From some poor herbalist, and armed with that
Came to this vault to die, and lie with Juliet.   290
Where are these enemies? Capulet, Montague,
See what a scourge is laid upon your hate,
With heaven using love to kill your joy.
And I, too quick to wink at all your strife
Have lost a pair of kinsmen. All are punished.   295

CAPULET
O brother Montague, give me your hand.
This is my daughter's recompense, no more
Can I demand.

MONTAGUE
                    But I can give you more,
For I will build her statue of pure gold,
And while Verona's still known by that name,   300
No figure shall attain the rate I set
As that for true and faithful Juliet.

CAPULET
As rich and by her side will Romeo's be,
Poor sacrifices to our enmity!

PRINCE ESCALUS
A gloomy peace is what this morning brings.   305
    The sun in sorrow will not show its face.
Let's go and hear more talk of these sad things.
    Some pardoned, others punished, case by case.
For never has a story had more woe
Than that of Juliet and her Romeo.   310

[Exit]

THE END

Endnotes

Act One

[1] Some editions have *cruel with the maids* replacing the ironic *civil* of the original.

[2] Some editions read "beauty to the same" (referring to "air" in the previous line).

[3] The original reads "Here's much to do with hate, but more with love." "To do" could mean "has to do with" or perhaps "commotion." It also could mean that hate keeps us busy but love even more so. My translation allows for the latter two senses and carries on Romeo's quibbling. Here's an alternate, less quibbling translation: "No doubt there's hate involved, but also love."

[4] The original lines 14-15 (*Earth hath swallowed all my hopes but she;/She's the hopeful lady of my earth*) are unrhymed (nine-syllable) headless lines, prompting some editors to omit them. My translation, in trying to mimic the meter as much as possible, also uses two headless, unrhymed lines.

[5] The original couplet in lines 32-33 (*Which one more view, of many, mine being one/May stand in number, though in reckoning none*) seems uninterpretable. Some scholars see the couplet as playing with a proverbial saying "one is no number" and thus none. I have Capulet ending with a riddle designed to encourage Paris to forget Juliet.

[6] The meaning of the original lines (*For I am proverb'd with a grandsire phrase/I'll be a candle-holder and look on—/The game was ne'er so fair, and I am done.*) is much disputed as is Mercutio's punning comeback (*Tut, dun's the mouse, the constable's own word*). I designed an exchange that is consistent with Romeo's behavior, preserves his punning on the word *game*, and allows Mercutio to tease him.

[7] The original couplet (*Take our good meaning, for our judgment sits/Five times in that ere once in our five wits*) has many interpretations. I take it to mean that too much punning stands in the way of efficient communication.

[8] Some editions prefer Quarto 2's "Direct my suit" because it allows for even more wordplay (quest, courtship, case).

Act Two

[1] The original reads "Young Abraham Cupid, he that shot so trim," variously taken to mean "Young, thieving Cupid/Young archer Cupid/Young, ancient Cupid/Young, auburn Cupid/Young beggar Cupid." They all scan if followed by "he who shot so true...." So take your pick. If Shakespeare simply intended an unlikely nickname, then try "Young Ambrose Cupid, he who shot so true...," which scans more easily for modern readers than "Abraham."

[2] The original is disputed. It is either *lazy-passing*, *lazy-pacing*, or *lazy-puffing*.

[3] In some editions, Romeo gets these lines (1-4) to close Scene 2. That passage would read:

> Sleep dwell within your eyes, peace in your breast!
> If I were sleep and peace, how sweet to rest!
> The gray-eyed morn smiles on the frowning night,
> Slicing the eastern clouds with streaks of light;
> And mottled darkness like a drunkard reels
> From daylight's path and Titan's fiery wheels.
> From here I'll go to my confessor's cell,
> His help I'll seek and my good luck I'll tell.

[4] Some editions rework the nurse's prose speech as blank verse with an irregular (and rather labored) meter.

Act Three

[1] Scholars cannot agree about the original's meaning "That runaways' eyes may wink...." The *New Variorum Edition* (1963) devotes 28 pages(!) of fine print to this dispute. I decided to move "runaway" up a few lines to describe the horses pulling the sun chariot and substitute "renegade" to link ironically with Romeo's status (still unknown to Juliet) and to suggest illicitly prying onlookers.

[2] John F. Andrews in the *Everyman Shakespeare* says Lady Capulet is addressing Juliet. Frank Kermode in the *Riverside Shakespeare* has her addressing Capulet. Kermode's analysis seems more likely to me. Even the bigoted, belligerent Lady Capulet would be likely to recoil at Capulet's awful characterization of their daughter.

Act Four

[1] Some editions add the line "I will not entertain so bad a thought."

[2] Lines 41-64 are often omitted on stage or delivered simultaneously. The First Quarto's stage direction says "All at once cry and wring their hands."

Sources

Editions of the Plays

The Arden Edition. 1980. Bryan Gibbons, ed. London and New York: Methuen.

The Bantam Shakespeare. 1988. David Benington, ed. New York: Bantam Books.

The Everyman Shakespeare. 1993. John F. Andrews, ed. London: J.M. Dent.

The New Folger Library Shakespeare. 1992. Barbara A. Mowat and Paul Werstine, eds. New York: Washington Square Press.

A New Variorum Edition. 1963. Horace Howard Furness, ed. New York: Dover Publications, Inc.

The Oxford Shakespeare. 2000. Jill L. Levinson, ed. Oxford: Oxford University Press.

Riverside Shakespeare. 1997. Boston and New York: Houghton Mifflin Company.

Shakespeare: Major Plays and the Sonnents. 1948. G. B. Harrison, ed. New York: Harcourt, Brace and World, Inc.

Other Sources

Crystal, David and Ben Crystal. *Shakespeare's Words: A Glossary and Language Companion*. 2002. London: Penguin Books.

Compact Edition of the Oxford English Dictionary. 1971. Oxford University Press.

Onions, C.T. *A Shakespeare Glossary.* 1986. Revised and enlarged by Robert D. Eagleson.

Schmidt, Alexander. 1971. *Shakespeare Lexicon and Quotation Dictionary, Volumes 1 and 2.* New York: Dover Publications.

Weller, Phillip. 2001. *Romeo and Juliet Navigator.* Clicknotes.com: www.clicknotes.com/romeo/welcome. html.

Facts About Romeo and Juliet

Shakespeare's 12th play (or so)

Most likely first performed 1595-1596

2,101 blank verse lines, including
9 long and 47 short lines (according to *Shake-speare's Metrical Art* by George T. Wright)

1 brief song
3 sonnets
1 aubade (Act 3, Scene 5, lines 1-36)

About 13% prose

38 characters with lines plus the chorus

4 female characters with lines

24 scenes plus 2 choruses

The Internet Movie Database lists 34 films titled
Romeo and Juliet (or *Rome e Giulietta, Roméo et Juliette,* etc.) dating back to 1908.

Musical adaptations include:
operas by Vincenzo Bellini (1830)
and Charles Gounod (1867),
a dramatic symphony by Hector Berlioz (1839),
a symphonic poem by Tchaikovsky (1867),
a ballet by Sergei Prokofiev (1936),
and the musical *West Side Story*
by Leonard Bernstein, Jerome Robbins,
and Stephen Sondheim (1957).

Story Credit:
Masuccio Salernitano (1476)
Luigi da Porto (1530)
Matteo Bandello (1554)
Pierre Boaistuau (1559)
Arthur Brooke (1562)
William Painter (1567)
With additional material from
Ovid 's *Metamorphoses* (born 43 BC)
Boccaccio's *Decameron* (1349-1351)
and
Chaucer's *Troilus and Creseyede* (1380-86)

ENJOY SHAKESPEARE

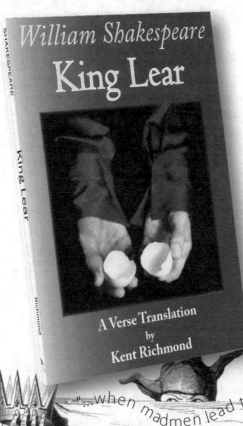

Two families torn by jealousy, ingratitude, and rage drive a kingdom to civil war and madness.

"...when madmen lead the blind."

ENJOY SHAKESPEARE brings Shakespeare's drama to life in the most complete verse translation available in English.

Order *King Lear* Online at
www.FullMeasurePress.com

ENJOY SHAKESPEARE

It came
by sea,
a love
that
sings
both
high
and
low.

ENJOY SHAKESPEARE brings Shakespeare's
comedy to life in the most complete
verse translation available in English.

**Order *Twelfth Night* at
www.FullMeasurePress.com**

ORDERING INFORMATION

Online Orders:	www.FullMeasurePress.com
Phone Orders:	(toll free) 1-888-569-4006
Fax Orders:	(562) 252-0250. Send this form.
email orders:	orders@FullMeasurePress.com
Postal Orders:	Full Measure Press
	P. O. Box 6294
	Lakewood, CA 90714-6294

ISBN	Title	Quantity/Price	
0-9752743-2-5	King Lear	____ x $9.95 =	
0-9752743-0-7	Romeo and Juliet	____ x $9.95 =	
0-9752743-0-9	Twelfth Night	____ x $9.95 =	
		Subtotal	
Add 8.25% sales tax if shipped to California			
U. S. shipping and handling for one book			$3.95
Add $1.00 for each additional book			
		Total	

Payment: ❏ Check   ❏ Credit Card

❏ Visa   ❏ MasterCard

Card Number: _____

Name on card: _____Exp. Date _____

Allow 3 weeks for postal orders.

Name: _____

Address: _____

City: _____ State: _____ ZIP: _____

Telephone: _____

email: _____